Andrew Louth is Professor Emeritus of Patristic and Byzantine Studies at Durham University and also Visiting Professor of Eastern Orthodox Theology at the Amsterdam Centre of Eastern Orthodox Theology (ACEOT), in the Faculty of Theology, the Free University, Amsterdam. He is also a priest of the Russian Orthodox Diocese of Sourozh (Moscow Patriarchate), serving the parish in Durham. He holds degrees from the University of Cambridge (MA), the University of Edinburgh (M.Th.) and the University of Oxford (DD). Before teaching at Durham, he taught at the University of Oxford and at Goldsmiths College, University of London.

He is the author of several books, including *The Origins of the Christian Mystical Tradition: Plato to Denys* (1981, second edition 2007), *Discerning the Mystery* (1983), *Denys the Areopagite* (1989), *Maximus the Confessor* (1996), *St John Damascene: Tradition and Originality in Byzantine Theology* (2002) and *Greek East and Latin West: the Church, AD 681–1071* (2007), as well as many articles.

Introducing

EASTERN ORTHODOX
THEOLOGY

Andrew Louth

IVP Academic

An imprint of InterVarsity Press
Downers Grove, Illinois

InterVarsity Press
P.O. Box 1400, Downers Grove, IL 60515-1426
Internet: www.ivpress.com
Email: email@ivpress.com

InterVarsity Press® is the book-publishing division of InterVarsity Christian Fellowship/USA®, a movement of students and faculty active on campus at hundreds of universities, colleges and schools of nursing in the United States of America, and a member movement of the International Fellowship of Evangelical Students. For information about local and regional activities, write Public Relations Dept., InterVarsity Christian Fellowship/USA, 6400 Schroeder Rd., P.O. Box 7895, Madison, WI 53707-7895, or visit the IVCF website at www.intervarsity.org.

Scripture quotations are the author's own translation.

Cover design: Cindy Kiple
Images: cross orthodox © Marek Kosmal/iStockphoto
church cupola © Anton Novikov/iStockphoto

USA ISBN 978-0-8308-4045-8 (print)
USA ISBN 978-0-8308-9535-9 (digital)
UK ISBN 978-0-281-06965-1 (print)
UK ISBN 978-0-281-06966-8 (digital)

Printed in the United States of America ∞

Library of Congress Cataloging-in-Publication Data

Louth, Andrew.
  Introducing Eastern Orthodox theology / Andrew Louth.
    pages cm
  Includes bibliographical references and index.
  ISBN 978-0-8308-4045-8 (paperback)
1. Orthodox Eastern Church—Doctrines. I. Title.
  BX320.3.L687 2013
  230'.19--dc23

                                                   2013031298

P	23	22	21	20	19	18	17	16	15	14	13	12	11	10	9	8	7	6	5
Y	33	32	31	30	29	28	27	26	25	24	23	22	21	20	19	18	17		

For Wendy

Contents

Contents

Preface

This book originated as a series of monthly public lectures delivered in the academic year 2011–2012 at the Amsterdam Centre for Eastern Orthodox Theology (ACEOT) in the Faculty of Theology in the Free University of Amsterdam, of which I was (and still am) a visiting professor. The lectures were, from the beginning, intended to be turned into the chapters of a book. I am very grateful for all those who turned up on Thursday evenings to listen to me, and to the discussions that took place following each lecture. I am especially grateful to Dr Michael Bakker, for inviting me to take up the visiting chair on the inauguration of the Centre in 2010. Various people have helped me to effect the transition from the ephemeral form of a lecture series to the more enduring form of a book, especially Fr John Behr, Wendy Robinson and Anna Zaranko. It still retains some of the informal tone of the original lectures; I hope the reader will be indulgent.

Andrew Louth
Feast of the Apostle Philip

Introduction:
who are the Eastern Orthodox?

Labels are sometimes a problem. Nobody wants to be labelled, and yet we use labels all the time, as a way of simplifying the world in which we live, a way of introducing some order and identity. Orthodox in the West have a particular problem with the labels others apply and they accept. 'Orthodox' by itself, in England and America, is usually taken to designate – outside a few, rather specialized contexts – Orthodox Judaism, as opposed to Conservative, Liberal or Reform Judaism. Some Orthodox use 'Christian Orthodox' to avoid that, or speak of them- selves as belonging to the 'Orthodox Church'. But there is no body called the 'Christian Orthodox Church', or even the 'Orthodox Church'; it is well known that there is the Greek Orthodox Church, the Russian Orthodox Church, the Romanian Orthodox Church and so on.

So who are the Orthodox? I have used what is probably still the most generally accepted term, 'Eastern Orthodox', though over the last century, the emigration of Orthodox from traditionally Orthodox countries to the West, their settlement here and the consequent attraction to their ranks of people with a cultural background that is entirely Western, means that there are now many members of the Orthodox Church who are uncomfortable with being thought 'Eastern', for there is nothing at all about them that is Oriental. So it seems to me that the best thing to do is to start by explaining whom I take the 'Eastern Orthodox' to be, rather than assuming that the label will not be misunderstood.

There seem to me to be three ways of approaching this question of identity and definition. The first is identifying those I am including under the title 'Eastern Orthodox', by providing a list – comprehensive, though not exhaustive. The second could be called historical: 'Eastern Orthodox' are who they are as the result of their history. Those of a Western background who have adopted Eastern Orthodoxy have, in some way, placed themselves in debt to that history. The third way might be to ask what is distinctive about Eastern Orthodoxy. I want to pursue each of these avenues one by one; in fact, I think, they will be found to lead one into another.

First of all, then, Eastern Orthodox means belonging to the family of Eastern Orthodox Churches, as opposed to the various families of Western Churches, and also to the Oriental Orthodox Churches. The Eastern Orthodox Churches, in this sense, are found to be various national groups. There are the Greek Orthodox: both in Greece itself, the Greek islands including Cyprus, but also the Greek diaspora, mostly to be found in Europe, the United States and Australia – the result of emigration from what is now Turkey, as well as Greece, and, especially in the case of Great Britain, from Cyprus – as well as Greek Orthodox under various ancient patriarchs (Antioch, Alexandria, Jerusalem). The leader of the Greek Orthodox is the Œcumenical Patriarch of Constantinople, now called Istanbul, in Turkey, where he still resides. (The title 'œcumenical' will be explained later.) There are also the Russian Orthodox, the Romanian Orthodox, the Bulgarian Orthodox, the Serbian Orthodox – all under patriarchs – as well as the Georgian Orthodox (under a Patriarch-Catholicos), and smaller churches in a variety of countries – for example, Albania, Estonia, Finland, Poland, the Czech lands and Slovakia. Many of these national groups also have significant numbers abroad, in the 'diaspora', mostly Western Europe and America, but elsewhere too.

All these national groups are in communion with one another, share the same faith (expressed in the decrees of the Œcumenical Councils – seven of them from Nicaea I in 325 to Nicaea II in 787), are ruled by the same body of Holy Canons and use the same Byzantine liturgy (generally in the local national language, or some older form of this: Greeks use Byzantine Greek, most Slavs Slavonic). The reasons for all this are historical: essentially that they all stem from the Orthodox Church of the Byzantine Empire (this is also true of the Georgian Orthodox Church, though in their case it is a little more complicated, as the Georgians embraced Christianity before the Byzantine Empire, and so must have had independent traditions, especially liturgical; however, over the centuries, their faithfulness to Byzantine Orthodoxy has entailed assimilation).

As well as the Eastern Orthodox Churches, there are the Churches often called the Oriental Orthodox Churches: these are Churches that refuse to accept some of the Œcumenical Councils endorsed by the Eastern Orthodox. Most accept the first three (Nicaea I – 325, Constantinople I – 381 and Ephesus – 431), but not the fourth (Chalcedon – 451) or any later ones; they include the Coptic Orthodox

Church (in Egypt), the Syrian Orthodox Church (Syria and India), the Armenian Orthodox Church (Armenia and Lebanon), the Ethiopian Orthodox Church and the Eritrean Orthodox Church – all have diasporas, some very widespread (especially in the cases of Armenia, Egypt and Syria): these are Churches that used to be called 'monophysite', because they were held to embrace the monophysite heresy, maintaining that in Christ divinity and humanity were fused into one. The Church of the East (mostly in Iran and the USA) accepts only the first two Œcumenical Councils (hence they used to be called 'Nestorian', after the patriarch of Constantinople who was condemned at the third Œcumenical Council, held in Ephesos in 431). The Oriental Churches – both the Oriental Orthodox Churches and the Church of the East – worship according to different liturgical rites from the Eastern Orthodox and govern their lives according to different canonical traditions.

Nonetheless, despite the apparently greater number of differences between the Eastern Orthodox and the Oriental Orthodox – compared with differences between Eastern Orthodox and Roman Catholics (who both, for instance, accept the first seven Œcumenical Councils, though the Roman Catholic Church accepts many more) – in many ways, Eastern Orthodox and Oriental Orthodox feel much closer to each other than either do to the West, and it has been accepted, at least at conferences of theologians, that the doctrinal differences are largely matters of misunderstanding.[1]

Why are these various Churches included in the 'list' of Eastern Orthodox Churches? The reasons for this are largely historical. So this leads us to the second, 'historical' avenue. Let us begin at the beginning with the band of disciples that followed the Lord Jesus Christ during his earthly ministry. They were, as far as we know, all Jews, and in the early decades after the death and resurrection of Christ the group that came to be called Christians (initially in Antioch: Acts 11.26) must have looked like a Jewish sect, who believed that in Jesus they had found the promised Messiah, or Christ ('anointed one').

However, Christians very soon came to realize that their 'good news', the 'gospel', was a worldwide message and they began to preach

---

[1] This was agreed at the official dialogue between Eastern and Oriental Orthodox delegates held at Chambésy in 1990. This agreement has, however, never been officially received or acted on by the Churches involved.

the gospel throughout the Mediterranean world (the Acts of the Apostles associates this realization with the apostles Peter and Paul). That worldwide missionary Church used Greek, the common language of the Mediterranean world (both in the East and in most of the West) – which is why, for example, the New Testament is in Greek. In fact, all the evidence for Christianity in the first two centuries outside the Semitic lands of its birth is of Greek Christianity, even in Rome; it is only in the third century that we find significant evidence of Latin Christianity, first in North Africa and Rome, and then in Spain and Gaul. One might think of Eastern Orthodox Christianity as the continuation of this worldwide missionary Church of the early centuries.

In the fourth century, the conversion of Constantine (312) led to the gradual adoption of Orthodox Christianity as the religion of the Roman Empire. As yet there was no split between East and West, only tensions. Constantine built a new capital for the newly Christian Empire, called Constantinople ('Constantine's city') or New Rome; soon the bishop there became the hierarch closest to the imperial throne in influence as well as proximity. Eventually he came to call himself the Œcumenical Patriarch, which expressed a sense of the priority of this see – alongside that of Rome, the ancient capital of the Roman or Byzantine Empire: the word 'œcumenical' is derived from the Greek word, *oikoumene*, the 'inhabited' (earth), which was the word the Roman (or Byzantine) Empire used, somewhat hubristically, to refer to its own territory; it conveys a sense of the 'worldwide' significance of the leader of the Church of Constantinople, 'New Rome'.

Before the ninth century, Christianity had begun to spread outside the immediate environs of the Byzantine Empire, mostly to the East, but also to Ireland (the conversion of England was regarded as the recovery of a lost part of the Roman Empire). In the ninth century, the expansion of Christianity led to the emergence of tensions between Western Christianity, focused on Rome and the Carolingian Empire, and Eastern Christianity, focused on Constantinople and the Byzantine Empire. This first manifested itself in Bulgaria. In the 860s Khan Boris decided to embrace Christianity and investigated the options of Greek East and Latin West. He opted for the East, and by the end of the century there was a branch of Byzantine Orthodoxy, worshipping and praying in Slavonic (had he opted for the Latin West, the Bulgarians would have worshipped and prayed in Latin, as in the rest of the West). This continued, and the Eastern Orthodox family of Churches uses (in principle) the vernacular.

The next important step was the conversion in the tenth century of Prince Vladimir of Kiev and the Rus', over whom he ruled. This led to the emergence of what has been called the Byzantine Commonwealth,[2] a loose grouping of countries that owed their faith to Byzantium and shared to some extent, at any rate, its political ideals: Bulgaria, the Rus' of Kiev to begin with, Serbia – in short the Slav world, together with the 'mother country', the Byzantine Empire.

The first half of the second millennium saw the Byzantine Empire gradually diminished by the advance of Muslim Turks. The only hope for the Byzantines was some alliance with the Christian West. By now, however, Greek East and Latin West had drifted apart and become increasingly estranged. Support against the Turks was only to be secured by union with the West, interpreted as submission to the Roman papacy. In this period the divisions between the Catholic West and the Orthodox East hardened. No union was achieved that was acceptable in the East, and in 1453 Constantinople itself fell to the Turks and became the capital of the Ottoman Empire. The Slavs of Rus', by this time beginning to free themselves from subjection to Muslim invaders – the Tatars, the 'Golden Horde' – began to assume the leadership of the Orthodox. The political centre of the newly emergent Russia was Moscow and in the next century or so, something like the Byzantine political polity was reproduced in Russia, with the Tsar fulfilling the role of the Emperor and the Patriarch of Moscow and all the Russias that of the Œcumenical Patriarch (though he never claimed that title). Meanwhile, the Œcumenical Patriarch became the leader of the Orthodox Christians in the Ottoman Empire, the 'Rum millet' (the people of [New] Rome). The Romanian Orthodox Church belongs to this later period of history as a Christian satellite of the Ottoman Empire under the Ottomans.

A final stage on the 'Historical Road of Eastern Orthodoxy' (to use the title of Fr Alexander Schmemann's book)[3] occurred in the nineteenth and twentieth centuries. The nineteenth century saw the gradual

---

[2] The title of a book by Dimitri Obolensky: *The Byzantine Commonwealth: Eastern Europe 500–1453* (London: Weidenfeld & Nicolson, 1971).

[3] Alexander Schmemann, *The Historical Road of Eastern Orthodoxy* (London: Holt, Rinehart & Winston, 1963).

liberation of various peoples from the Ottoman Empire – Greece, Serbia, Bulgaria – and their establishment as 'nations', with their own king and patriarch. The twentieth century saw the emigrations that caused the Orthodox diasporas: groups displaced by the break-up of the Ottoman Empire and the emergence of a secular state, Turkey, and those expelled from Russia as a result of the communist revolution and Lenin's exile of those intellectuals who refused to support communism, as well as many others who fled their homeland as a result of war and revolution throughout Europe. The presence in the West of these diasporas also changed Orthodoxy, as Orthodox Christians encountered the West and sought to understand the differences they found among many Christians who were sympathetic and welcoming.

Which leads to my third avenue: if we know who counts among the Eastern Orthodox, and something of their history, how are Eastern Orthodox Christians different from Western Christians? What makes them distinctive? This is more difficult to answer, especially in a Western context, where indications of distinctiveness are sometimes part of the labels: for example, Lutheran, Calvinist, Wesleyan Methodist, labels all indicating a defining individual theologian (not necessarily thought of as a 'founder').

The label 'orthodox' does not work like that. In current parlance, it has two valencies: it either suggests correctness (orthodox being derived from two Greek roots, and meaning 'correct opinion') or – very commonly – what people used to think, or still think, with the suggestion that this opinion has had its day (as when one speaks of the [current] orthodoxy about some topic). That may give some clue to the meaning of Orthodoxy for the Orthodox themselves, for it suggests that correct opinion or belief is something to be valued. It suggests commitment to the importance of dogma: Orthodoxy involves acceptance of dogmatic truths, that is, truths that are important and have been defined, in the case of Eastern Orthodoxy, by the Seven Œcumenical Councils which are revered in the Orthodox Church. But, as we shall see in more detail in this book, while dogma is important, in the sense that there are matters about which it is important to be right (or perhaps better: matters about which it is dangerous to be wrong), what this really means is that there is truth – about God, his engagement with the world that he created, and especially the Incarnation in which he united himself with his creation – that is not simply a matter of opinion. It can be defined, though definition in such matters is less a question of delineating something exactly, than of preventing misunderstanding that is all too easy. Fundamentally that is the case, because such truth is not so much a matter of getting things right, as genuine encounter with the Person of Christ, witnessed in the Scriptures, safeguarded in the definitions of Church Councils, and experienced in the sacraments and the Church.

You might say that there is nothing very distinctive about this; many Christians would embrace such an orthodoxy. I would respond that this is indeed so, that Orthodox Christians see themselves as committed to the truth of the Councils and the creeds, a truth that unites Christians, not one that divides them; Orthodoxy has an inclusive distinctiveness, it is not a peculiarity. That something like this is true is indicated, it seems to me, by the enormous popularity writings like C. S. Lewis's *Mere Christianity* have found in traditionally Orthodox countries.[4] *Mere Christianity* presents Christianity as the heart of what all Christians believe, and was itself the fruit of a movement among Western, mostly English-speaking, mostly lay, Christians, who sought to restore a sense of the value of traditional orthodoxy – the traditional faith of most Christians – in the face of a 'liberalism' that seemed to misunderstand and weaken traditional Christian teaching about God the Trinity, creation and Incarnation, sin and redemption.

If there is anything distinctive about Eastern Orthodoxy, it is not that it is an exotic belief, remote from what Western Christians believe Rather, its distinctiveness is to be found in the *way* in which the traditional faith of Christians is upheld among the Orthodox. For Orthodoxy sees its faith as expressed, and tested, in prayer and worship.

Many Christians would assent to that, but there have been influential movements within Western Christianity that have sought to express Christianity in some comprehensive philosophy – the scholasticism of the Western Middle Ages is a striking example – or make some particular doctrine the article by which the Church stands or falls – as Luther did with the doctrine of justification by faith. In reaction against that, in the West, other movements have sought to reduce Christianity to a non-dogmatic devotionalism – implicitly in certain

---

[4] C. S. Lewis, *Mere Christianity* (London: Fontana Books, 1959).

strands of Western medieval mysticism, or explicitly in pietism. But for Eastern Orthodoxy it is in prayer and worship of God that our faith is defined and refined: a God who created the world and loves it, whose love is expressed in his identifying himself with his creation, and especially the human creation, made in his image, through the Incarnation and the cross, a love that is manifested in its transfiguring power through the resurrection. The centrality of prayer and worship prevent us from narrowing down our faith to some human construction, however magnificent.

If there is any reason why Eastern Orthodoxy has found this way of confessing the Faith, it could be because the way of Eastern Orthodoxy has led through persecution and martyrdom: in every century there have been Christians of the Orthodox communion who have faced persecution – throughout the whole Christian world in the first centuries, and then while living under the rule of Islam, and in the last century atheist communism. In all these centuries it has been faithfulness to the prayer and worship of the Church that has enabled the Church to survive. Often it was only in gathering together for prayer and worship that Orthodox Christians were able to express their faith, and frequently such gathering together was subject to harassment – a harassment sometimes as severe as any persecution. And they found that that was enough, that faithfulness in prayer and worship, in celebrating the divine liturgy, in belonging to the saints of all ages and joining our prayers with theirs, and then living out, as fully as they could, lives formed by that worship: all this proved to be in truth the touchstone of their faith. The experience of martyrdom and persecution has been the crucible in which Orthodox Christians have found their faith refined.

1

Thinking and doing, being and praying: where do we start?

Well, where *do* we start? In *Alice in Wonderland*, the White Rabbit is advised by the King of Hearts: 'Begin at the beginning . . . and go on till you come to the end: then stop.' That sounds like good advice, but how are we to apply it? Many accounts of the Christian faith adopt the order of the creed, beginning with God the Father and continuing through the Son, and then the Spirit, to the Church and eternal life. That makes some sort of sense, but it seems to me to beg a question, one that we need to face up to. For if there is one thing we know about God the Father, it is that he is unknowable. 'No one has ever seen God' (John 1.18). 'You cannot see my face', God says to Moses, 'for man shall not see me and live' (Exod. 33.22): this warning is repeated throughout the Old Testament, though usually in contexts where God actually is 'seen' or apprehended in some way (as with Moses). How can we start with God the Father, if we cannot know him?

This is a question we can pursue in various ways. Perhaps this means that we start with God, not as knowing him, but as standing before a mystery that is, and will remain, beyond our understanding. In the Liturgy of St John Chrysostom, at the beginning of the anaphora, we justify our attempts to worship God by saying: 'for you are God, ineffable, incomprehensible, invisible, inconceivable, ever existing, eternally the same'.[1] Our worship is a response to an unfathomable mystery. In a sense, if we start there we shall never proceed: for once we glimpse the unfathomable mystery of God, we shall never drag ourselves away. Or maybe we shall proceed, but constantly find ourselves drawn back to the inexhaustibility of this mystery that God is.

---

[1] *The Divine Liturgy of our Father among the Saints John Chrysostom* (Oxford: Oxford University Press, 1995), 31.

But if we do proceed, there is another problem. If we posit God and then consider him as Creator, source of all values, especially moral, and continue, as we consider the creed, to think of the Incarnation of God the Son, all that led up to that, all that has followed from it, the paschal mystery of the death and resurrection of Christ, the outpouring of the Spirit, the birth of the Church, then what is it that we are doing? It looks like an objective list of persons and events that we simply relate.

But how can that be, how do we know that it is like that? The creed, we need to remind ourselves, is not a list of things to believe, it is itself a liturgical text, belonging, first of all, to the baptismal liturgy. It summarizes the faith that the newly baptized Christian is embracing; it is the culmination of a process of learning about the faith, and beginning to practise what it requires, in a doubtless stumbling way; it opens up to the new life of the baptized, a life that draws its sustenance from the Eucharist, which in Orthodox practice is immediately celebrated after the baptismal liturgy, or rather as the final part of the rite of initiation. Both the paths we have just sketched converge: if to acknowledge God is to acknowledge his unknowability and stand before him in awe; if the creed is part of our initiation into a life, not a summary of things to be believed, then in both cases we do not stand over against God; rather, we are finding ourselves caught up in the divine presence and the divine activity, and trying to make sense of it. It is something of what is involved in that, how that presence and that activity are felt by us, that I want to explore in this chapter.

When I gave the course of lectures from which this book is derived, I called it a 'personal introduction'. There were two reasons for that. First, I claim no authority for what I am saying. I am keen to stand in the tradition of the Church, and hope that I do. But I am not a bishop, I do not have the grace 'rightly to discern the word of the truth'.[2] Second, my presentation is personal; it is how I see it. Furthermore, what I see is personal: it is the result of a personal engagement (doubtless flawed), and demands personal engagement. I am not presenting something to you that is independent of either what I see or what you see; I am suggesting that you look with me at something and I hope that you will see something of what it is that engages me.

---

[2] 2 Tim. 2.15: applied to 'the episcopacy of the Orthodox' in the anaphorae of both St John Chrysostom and St Basil.

If that is so, then various conclusions follow. To change the metaphor, I am inviting you on a journey. I can point out various things that we encounter on the way, perhaps even warn you against some paths that I fear will simply mislead you; but the journey is yours – it will involve your commitment, your struggle. This is why I called this first chapter 'Thinking and doing, being and praying'. An introduction to Eastern Orthodox theology, as I understand it, may well involve learning various facts and dates, terminology and concepts, but at its heart it is an introduction to a way of life.

I am a priest, and I am used to preaching, but I hope that you will not find this book too much like a sequence of homilies. However, there is no complete break between what I do as I try to lead my congregation deeper into their discipleship of Christ and what I am doing in this book, as I try to sketch out what Eastern Orthodox theology involves. There will be a difference of emphasis, a difference of balance, but not a complete difference, because I do not think one can present theology in the Orthodox tradition without making clear that at its heart there is an engagement, ultimately an engagement with God. 'Thinking and doing, being and praying': these are fundamental human activities. It is the case, I would suggest, that we do not exactly learn to do these things – we engage in these simply by being human – what happens is that we learn what is involved in doing these things.

For this reason, several movements in twentieth-century philosophy are at some level deeply sympathetic to what I am suggesting here. Both the hermeneutical tradition associated with Heidegger and the rather different tradition associated with Wittgenstein have in common a conviction that we do not start out ignorant, and then by means of 'philosophy' come to a knowledge of the world. Rather, we already know the world in some sense, simply by living in it, and what philosophy does is help us to reflect on what is involved in that knowledge of the world. So it is with theology: thinking and doing, being and praying, are activities we all engage in at some level or another. The questions about how we are to live, what it means to be, how we engage with the world, how we engage with what seems to transcend the world: we can hardly live without asking these questions. So we are already theologians. Orthodox theology takes us along a path, marked out by tradition, that helps us in our continuing grappling with these questions.

Standing before the mystery of God

I began by asking: where do we start? and reflected on the paradox that we seem to start from a place of unknowing, not in the sense of ignorance – as if we started off with little knowledge and found that it increased – but in a more fundamental sense – starting off with an awareness that the One we seek to know is beyond any capacity we might have for knowing.

I suggested that we find ourselves standing before the mystery of a God who is beyond knowledge. And it is from this point that I want to indicate our next steps. We stand before God. We are always standing before God, for there is no place where God is not, as opposed to a place where he is: wherever we are we are before God. But there are places where, from a human perspective, the presence of God is more apparent to us, places where it is less easy for us to forget that God is here.

These places are many and various, and our sensitivity to them is in part a matter of our own upbringing and history. There is, for example, a very strong tradition – in many geographical and historical cultures – that mountains are places where God is encountered. The reason is partly because mountains are not easily amenable to human modification. Other places are more easily covered over with what humans have done to make themselves at home in them, but mountains – and rivers, and the sea – are resistant to human fashioning. One is already detached from what humans make of things; one is already open to the power that lies behind everything. We have a sense of the transcendent, as we put it, a sense of the divine. The poet, T. S. Eliot, put it well when he said of Little Gidding (the holiness of which has to do with historical events) that it is a place '[w]here prayer has been valid'.[3]

I want to suggest that the first step in the pursuit of Orthodox theology, in coming to know God in accordance with the Orthodox tradition, is the rediscovery of this sense of standing before God (standing is a more customary attitude for prayer in the Eastern Orthodox tradition than kneeling), and pre-eminently standing before God in church. This is the place where people pray, where the liturgical services are held, a place surrounded and defined by icons.

---

[3] T. S. Eliot, *Four Quartets* (London: Faber & Faber, 1944), 36.

It is filled with the evidence of human worship of God – the singing of sacred song, the sight of sacred architecture and garments, the smell of the incense, the touching of sacred things – icons and relics – and the sense of other people standing there before God. This is where we start.

Many who stand in such a place are already committed to the faith being celebrated. Yet you do not have to believe to go into a church; you can stand there alongside people who do believe, next to people you know, or even out of curiosity. But here is where theology begins, according to the Orthodox tradition, at least as I understand it: in a mysterious togetherness, mediated by silence (chattering during the services is not encouraged, even if it is sometimes difficult to prevent), full of sounds and smells that seem to interpret this silence rather than dissolve it. And here, too, it may end – caught up in the presence of God, open to his spirit, bearing before him in our hearts the concerns of those with whom we have to do. If we seek to understand it, we shall only ever understand in part. But there is something to understand, and such understanding is what we might well call theology.

Approaching theology

There are lots of things that further such understanding that we call theology, and in the rest of this book we shall explore some of them. What I want to do in this chapter is give some sense of orientation. What is it that furthers theological understanding and how are we to approach it?

What is involved in theological understanding in the Christian tradition, and especially the Orthodox tradition, is fairly familiar. There are the Scriptures. There is reflection on the Scriptures by those we often call theologians, but also by others to whom we rarely extend the title. There are controversies that have arisen over the interpretation of the tradition, and the attempts to solve these controversies that have become established in the Orthodox tradition, notably the synods or councils, especially those called 'œcumenical'. There is a living voice in the Church, articulating the tradition in the different historical circumstances in which the Church has found itself, a voice that is not merely human, but safeguarded and inspired by God's help or grace – we hear this living voice in the bishops, who have the

5

grace 'rightly to discern the word of the truth'. There is also the prayer of the Church: the liturgical prayers of the divine liturgy and the offices of the Church, where what we believe is spelt out in the words we use as we turn to God. And there are lives of prayer – most prominently the lives of monks and ascetics, but just as validly the lives of those in whom we can see a living out of the life in Christ – and these lives have authority, even though it is not provided for in a formal way, as is the authority of bishops. Nevertheless, retrospectively, in the case of the saints, these lives have acquired a fundamental importance in the history of the Orthodox Church.

This can become a list: scriptural exegesis, patristic theology, the theology of the councils (and alongside this the tradition of the Holy Canons, spelling out aspects of the Christian life), Church history and rebuttal of heresy, the role of the hierarchy, the place of the monastic order and the role of prayer (which includes the way in which liturgy defines meaning – in the case of both sacraments and the great feasts of the Church – as well as the role of those whose 'prayer has been valid', the saints and martyrs, and the way in which devotion to the saints has been expressed through the cult of relics and the development of iconography). This list, however, can become something quite different, more like labelling the limbs and organs of a body, so that there is an organic relationship between all the elements thus labelled. It is this that I want to explore briefly now.

Encountering Christ

There seem to me to be two elements in seeing how all these different factors come to form a single organic whole. On the one hand, and fundamentally, there is the realization that all this relates to Christ. The Scriptures are not primarily sources of reliable – still less infallible – information about religious matters; rather, Christ stands at their centre; they bear witness to him. The books of the Old Testament tell of God's ways with the world and humans, at the centre of which there is the history of the people of Israel, among whom the Son of God became incarnate as the fulfilment of the promises to Israel and the hopes of all humanity. The New Testament contains the apostolic witness to Christ, to his birth, ministry, death, resurrection and ascension, and the pouring out of the Holy Spirit on the Church and the whole human race. But all this is more than record: it is through the Scriptures that Christ continues to encounter human kind; to read the Bible as Scripture is to be open to encounter with Christ. The same applies *mutatis mutandis* to the writings of the Fathers, the history of the Church and its councils, the lives of the saints: all these are ways of encountering Christ, or of understanding the lineaments of such an encounter. And what makes this a possibility is prayer; it is prayer that creates beings capable of hearing the voice of Christ.

These lead us to the other element involved, for prayer to Christ and openness to his voice takes us back to the point we started with – the mystery of God. For that mystery is not simply an intellectual mystery; it is something much deeper. As we shall see again and again in the course of this book, encounter with Christ entails opening ourselves to an inner transformation, to a fundamental repentance.

Mother Thekla, a Russian nun who died at a great age in summer 2011, once wrote about what her monastery was engaged in as it sought (through publishing: the immediate context of this quotation) to express the Orthodox tradition in its English environment, and spoke of 'the one innermost battle-cry of the monastery, the austere demand of refusing to discuss what is not lived, and the impossibility of living this ourselves: back into the revolving wheel of repentance: Face God, not man'.[4] This sense of theology as rooted in experience, and yet the idea that this experience is beyond us, so that we are constantly pushed back to repent, to turn again to God: this seems to me absolutely central to the Orthodox experience of theology, of coming to know God.

There are two elements? – dimensions? – here: we stand before God and listen and we stand before God and we speak, or try to. These two dimensions are held together in various ways. We stand before God, as part of the body of Christ, the Church: we hear the voice of Christ, and we respond *with* the voice of Christ. This is very evident in the Christian use of the psalms: these are words that we hear, they are also words that we use. Many of the Fathers suggest that in both cases it is in union with Christ that we hear and pray the psalms: we both pray with Christ and we pray to Christ; we both

---

[4] Mother Thekla, *The Monastery of the Assumption: A History* (Library of Orthodox Thinking, pamphlet no. 8; Whitby: Greek Orthodox Monastery of the Assumption, 1984), 16.

hear Christ and we speak with his voice. It seems to me that this applies more generally in the Christian use of the Scriptures: we hear the Scriptures, addressed to us, but at the same time, the Scriptures provide us with words, images, feelings, even concepts and ideas, that we use when, in Christ, we address God.

The Scriptures

Let me try and develop this more specifically: How do we interpret Scripture in the Orthodox tradition?[5] How does the Orthodox interpretation of Scripture differ from the way Scripture is interpreted by other Christians, by scholars? What is the role of the Fathers, of Church Councils, of the prayers of the Church in her various offices?

It is sometimes said that Orthodox Christians kiss the Gospel Book, but they don't read it. I hope that is not true, but it is certainly true that we do not only read the Gospel, the Gospel Book is an object of veneration: it is carried in procession at the Little Entrance, its binding is usually decorated with icons, of the resurrection and of the cross – there are examples of Gospel Books with marvellous illuminations throughout. This is not irrelevant, or superfluous, for the Gospel Book is seen as an icon of Christ. St Theodore the Studite, in the second stage of the Iconoclast controversy, spoke of icons as 'written in gold', compared with the Gospel that was 'written in ink'. The comparison works both ways: just as an icon is venerated, because it images forth the one depicted and so provides access to the one depicted, so the Gospel, through what is written in it, provides us with access to the one who is the Gospel: Christ, Emmanuel, God-with-us. It is still 'writing in ink', which needs to be interpreted, but it is important because it discloses Christ, it invites us to an encounter with Christ.

The Orthodox approach to the Scriptures endeavours to keep a balance between these two dimensions. The patient work of scholarship is important. The Bible is a collection of books written over hundreds, even thousands of years. They were written and rewritten in particular historical circumstances, and understanding those historical circumstances will help us to read them in an appropriate

---

[5] For another attempt at discussing the interpretation of Scripture in the Orthodox tradition, see my 'Inspiration of the Scriptures', *Sobornost* 31.1 (2009), 29–44.

way. The text of the scriptural books themselves is not something we can take for granted. There are a host of manuscripts, with differing readings, and there are scholarly methods for seeking to establish the original meaning.

All this is useful, and there is no reason why an Orthodox Christian should ignore it. But it is not the whole story. Scholarly interpretation has been governed by an overriding concern to establish the original text and meaning. But there are many circumstances in which this is either not appropriate or not the whole story. For the Scriptures do not simply belong to their original context: they have been read and re-read over the centuries. When we venerate the Book of the Gospels we are acknowledging it as something that belongs to the present: it bodies forth Christ now. When we read the passages from the Gospels, we are not simply reading some text that we can trace back to the first century, based on an oral tradition that goes back to events in the life of Christ and those who were there: we are reading the Gospel, confident that we can discern Christ's voice speaking to us now. The recognition that we are dealing with a living text, a text that, in some sense, is contemporary, not just to the time of its composition, but to the time of its reading, suggests considerations that even the driest scholarship should be able to take into account.

Take, for example, the book of the Psalms: What is it? It is a collection of poetry, belonging to a wide range of dates, written by individuals of whom we now know nothing, or even in some cases by individuals whom we can identify – King David, as tradition has it for several of the psalms (the evidence is contradictory, for clearly it is possible to have different views about the provenance of the inscriptions to the psalms, which differ between the Hebrew and the Greek texts). But it is also a collection of religious poetry that was used in the worship of the Temple – certainly in the case of the second Temple (built c. 520 BC and – after a period of desecration under Antiochos IV Epiphanes – finally destroyed by the Romans in AD 70), the temple in which Jesus worshipped, and probably in the case of the first Temple, built during the reign of King Solomon and destroyed by the Babylonians c. 586 BC. Used in that context, the psalms related to the temple services, and helped people to relate their own concerns to the services in which they participated.

Furthermore, the psalms constitute a body of religious poetry used in the Jewish synagogue after the destruction of the Temple: here, yet

9

another context elicited further meaning. And the Psalter has become the song book of the Christian Church, and that in a host of ways, from the use of particular psalms in particular contexts – for instance, the use of Psalm 103,[6] a psalm of creation, at Vespers in the Byzantine office – to the recitation of the whole Psalter on a regular basis, which became the practice in monasticism, both in the East and in the West, in the East by dividing up the Psalter into 20 sections of roughly equal length called *kathismata* ('sittings'), which are distributed over the monastic office on a weekly basis.

Given that variety of uses, what a particular psalm means cannot be restricted to some supposed original use by the one who composed it – a context that is no more than conjectural, anyway. For a Christian interpretation of the psalms, it would make sense to pay attention to the Christian use of the Psalter, which does not exclude other interpretations.

Orthodox use of the Scriptures

There is, so far as I can tell, no real consensus over how the Scriptures are to be interpreted in the Orthodox world; many departments of Old Testament and New Testament in faculties of theology in Greece, Russia and Romania, for example, seem to approach the Scriptures in much the same way as Catholic and Protestant faculties in the West, perhaps with an inclination to be conservative in their adoption of scholarly approaches. There is a sense that patristic interpretation of the Scriptures is important, but no systematic attempt to put that into practice. Perhaps there is no systematic way of incorporating patristic interpretation, perhaps we should be looking for something else. It does, however, seem to me that the liturgical use of Scripture should have some kind of priority in the Orthodox Church, though what this means still needs to be worked out. But it would involve paying attention to how the Scripture is presented in the lectionary. Even a brief glance at that (all we can do now) provides some indications.

---

[6] Throughout, I shall use the numeration of the Psalms found in the Septuagint (and the Latin Vulgate); except for Psalms 1–8 and 146–150, the numeration found in the Septuagint (lxx) is mostly one less than the numeration found in the Hebrew Bible (and most English Bibles), so Ps. 103 (lxx) = Psalm 104 (Hebrew Bible).

The lectionary was clearly put together with some care, though we know virtually nothing about how it was done or the principles of selection, apart from what can be deduced from the lectionary as we have it (which is very ancient, and reached its final form in the second half of the first millennium). Broadly speaking, the 'Apostle' (the Acts and the epistles of Paul and other apostles) and the Gospels are read sequentially; no attempt is made to select themes (except on feast days). That suggests that the New Testament can be left to speak for itself. However, within this sequential reading, the readings on Saturdays and Sundays select the more important passages (though it is not clear what the criteria were for such selection), while the rest of the week we have a sequential reading of what is left.

The sequence starts on Easter Sunday when the beginning of the Acts of the Apostles and the Prologue of John's Gospel are read, and the reading of Acts and the fourth Gospel continues throughout the 50 days to Pentecost. After Pentecost, we begin to read the epistles of Paul and the Gospel of Matthew. In the Greek practice, after the Feast of the Lifting Up of the Holy Cross (14 September) we turn to the Gospel of Luke; while the Gospel of Mark is read on the Sundays of Lent (and on the weekdays towards the end of the 'Matthaean' period, when passages from the first Gospel run out). The readings from the epistles of Paul, then James, Peter and John, continue until the end of the pre-Lenten period. During Lent, there are readings from the New Testament only at the weekends, when the divine liturgy is celebrated (from Hebrews for the Apostle, from Mark, as we have seen, for the Gospel); on weekdays the readings are from the Old Testament: Isaias at the Sixth Hour, and Genesis and Proverbs at Vespers – Ezekiel, Exodus and Job during Holy Week. In addition, on major feasts, there are readings (generally three) from the Old Testament at Vespers, and readings from the Apostle and Gospel at the divine liturgy: they are chosen for their relevance to the feast being celebrated.

There seem to be several principles behind all this. The New Testament (apart from the Apocalypse) is read in full, and always read in conjunction with the divine liturgy: there is clearly some link between celebrating the liturgy in remembrance of Christ and reading from the New Testament. The Old Testament, in contrast, is read very selectively, and read at the offices, mostly at Vespers. Vespers, in the Byzantine rite (and in the Western rite until the reforms of the last century), celebrates the beginning of the liturgical day, following

11

the Jewish practice to which the account of creation in Genesis bears witness: each day of creation is presented as 'evening and morning', in that order. Vespers, then, looks forward to the breaking of the new day, and the Old Testament is read then because it, too, from a Christian perspective, looks forward to the rising of the daystar, Christ as God incarnate.

Furthermore, the Old Testament is read following the text of the Greek Bible. That sounds curiously innocent, but I think there may be more to it than meets the eye. It is well known that the New Testament, for the most part, cites the Old Testament according to the Greek text of the Septuagint (the pre-Christian Jewish translation of the Hebrew Bible into Greek), and thereafter the Septuagint became the authoritative text for virtually all Christians (even Jerome's preference for *Hebraica Veritas* was much qualified, in practice, by the experience of the Church).[7]

But the situation is more complicated than that. In the second century there were several other Jewish translations, presumably intended to rescue the text of the Old Testament from the Christian use based on the Septuagint. In the third century, Origen gathered the various translations together and laid them out in six columns, in a vast work of scholarship called the *Hexapla*. Its purpose was not, as is often asserted, to enable Origen to establish a text more correct than that of the Septuagint, but rather to lay bare the richness of meaning contained in the Scriptures of the Old Testament. Passages from the other columns of the *Hexapla* found their way into Christian copies of the Septuagint – so-called 'Hexaplaric' readings – and it is these readings that we often find in patristic commentaries on Scripture, as well as in the texts included in the services in the Byzantine liturgy. The consequence of this, it seems to me, is profound: there is no 'authoritative text' of the Old Testament for Orthodox Christians; instead, there is a long process of exploring everything there might be in the witness of the Hebrew Scriptures to the coming of Christ.

---

7 The importance of the LXX as the Christian Old Testament has achieved some recognition in recent biblical scholarship: See Mogens Müller, *The First Bible of the Church: A Plea for the Septuagint* (Journal for the Study of the Old Testament. Supplement Series, 206; Sheffield: Sheffield Academic Press, 1996); Martin Hengel, *The Septuagint as Christian Scripture* (Edinburgh: T. & T. Clark, 2002). For Jerome, see Adam Kamesar, *Jerome, Greek Scholarship and the Hebrew Bible* (Oxford: Clarendon Press, 1993); C. T. R. Hayward, *Jerome's Hebrew Questions on Genesis* (Oxford: Clarendon Press, 1995).

A Greek 'Old Testament' is not what it seems. The one published in Greece by Zoe has modified some version of the Septuagint by assimilating the text to that found in the service books, when such passages are used – clearly a rather hit-and-miss process;[8] while the Church of Greece has published, under its authority, the scholarly version of the Septuagint prepared by Rahlfs which seeks to establish an 'original' text and in its conjectural readings, sometimes omits passages universally found in the MSS and important in the texts of the Church – for instance the words which begin the anaphora of St Basil: 'The One who is, Master, Lord' (cf. Jer. 1.6 LXX).

What does all this add up to? It suggests to my mind an attitude to Scripture that sees it not as some flat collection of infallible texts about religious matters, but rather as a body of witness of varying significance – some clearly crucial, as witnessing very directly to Christ, others less important (though never of no importance), as their witness to Christ is more oblique. And the criteria for importance are bound up in some way with the way the Church has taken them up into her experience. There is a hierarchy, a shape: the Gospel Book at the centre, the Apostle flanking it, and then a variety of texts from the Old Testament, generally accessed not through some volume called the Bible, but from extracts contained in the liturgical books, along with other texts: songs, passages from the Fathers and so on. The Scriptures then have a kind of shape, a shape that relates to our experience of them.

The Fathers, Councils, liturgical prayer

I would like to say something similar about the other 'authorities' we consult in Orthodox theology: the Fathers, the Councils and the prayers of the Church. There is no question of making the Fathers, or any selection of them, infallible authorities. They disagree with one another over all sorts of issues, and we should beware of trying to iron out the differences between them. What we should hear from the chorus of the Fathers is a rich harmony, not a thin unison.

Similarly with the decisions of the councils, especially the Holy Canons. Although the canons have been collected together, time and again, there is no disguising the fact that they were issued by councils

---

[8] *I Agia Graphi* (15th edn, Athens: Ekdosis Adelfotitos Theologon I «Zoi», 1999).

for particular reasons, in particular contexts. If we put them all together, we shall not find in them detailed guidance on all the problems that face us nowadays. Some Orthodox thinkers have made capital of this, arguing that the open texture of the canons makes room for a creative freedom as we seek to live the Gospel – and I would agree with them.[9]

Perhaps most important of all, aside from the Scriptures, are the prayers and songs of the Church, which take us into the experience of the sacred mysteries. It seems to me, for instance, that the texts of the songs that we sing at the Feast of the Dormition of the Mother of God take us more closely and assuredly to the meaning of the feast than any dogmatic definition could ever do. Take, for instance, the kontakion for the dormition:

> Neither tomb nor death overpowered the Mother of God, unsleeping in her prayers, unfailing hope in intercession; for as Mother of Life she has been taken over into life by him who dwelt in her ever-virgin womb.[10]

Here we learn that the mystery of the dormition is the mystery of intercession, intercession that is constantly life-giving, for life has overcome death, and in her death we see the barrier between death and life quite transparent.

I want to end this chapter with a quotation from one of the greatest Russian thinkers and theologians of the last century, Fr Pavel Florensky. Towards the end of the first letter in his *Pillar and Ground of the Truth*, he has this to say:

> the life of the Church is assimilated and known only through life – not in the abstract, not in a rational way. If one must nevertheless apply concepts to the life of the Church, the most appropriate concepts would be not juridical and archaeological ones but biological and aesthetic ones. What is ecclesiality? It is a new life, life in the Spirit. What is the criterion of the rightness of this life? Beauty. Yes, there is a special beauty of the spirit, and, ungraspable by logical formulas, it is at the

---

[9] In different ways: see N. Afanasiev, 'The Church's Canons: Changeable or Unchangeable?', in *Tradition Alive: On the Church and the Christian Life in our Time: Readings from the Eastern Church* (ed. Michael Plekon; Lanham, MD: Rowman & Littlefield, 2003), 31–45; C. Yannaras, *The Freedom of Morality* (Crestwood, NY: St Vladimir's Seminary Press, 1984), 175–93.

[10] Translation from *Liturgy of St John Chrysostom*, 80.

same time the only true path to the definition of what is orthodox and what is not orthodox.

The connoisseurs of this beauty are the spiritual elders, the *startsy*, the masters of the 'art of arts', as the holy fathers call asceticism. The *startsy* were adept at assessing the quality of spiritual life. The Orthodox taste, the Orthodox temper, is felt but it is not subject to arithmetical calculation. Orthodoxy is shown, not proved. That is why there is only one way to understand Orthodoxy: through direct orthodox experience . . . to become Orthodox, it is necessary to immerse oneself all at once in the very element of Orthodoxy, to begin living in an Orthodox way. There is no other way.[11]

---

[11] Pavel Florensky, *The Pillar and Ground of the Truth: An Essay in Orthodox Theodicy in Twelve Letters* (trans. Boris Jakim; Princeton, NJ: Princeton University Press, 1997), 8–9.

2

Who is God? The doctrine of the Holy Trinity

Who is Christ?

At the heart of Christianity is the cross, and the One who was executed on it: the Lord Jesus Christ. But who was this man? – for whatever else we believe about him, he was certainly a man. The earliest witnesses to Jesus, which we find in the Gospels, and the rest of the New Testament, make all sorts of suggestions: a prophet, 'The Prophet', Son of Man, Son of God, Word of God, the Wisdom and Power of God. How Christians and the Church followed up these suggestions I shall pursue (or at least refer to) later on in this book. But for now I want to make a much simpler observation. The Gospels present Jesus as a teacher, a wonderworker, one who came to be considered (in ways not really explored in the Gospels, save for his opposition to those called 'Pharisees') a threat: a threat to the Jewish religion, in some sense, and beyond that a political threat (that he was crucified makes clear that the execution was performed by the Roman occupiers of Palestine).

But how did Jesus think of himself? In what way did he want to be remembered? As a prophet and teacher, he preached; parables seem to have characterized his teaching. But what did he teach? There is not a great deal in his teaching that cannot be paralleled in contemporary or earlier Jewish teaching. Even the twofold command – to love God and to love one's neighbour – is presented in St Luke's Gospel, not as Jesus' teaching, but as a summary of the Law provided by a Jewish lawyer in answer to Jesus' question (Luke 10.27). Jesus is not presented as a great teacher with a new message: he speaks with a new authority, but what he preaches is the message of the Law and the Prophets. Jesus is not a philosopher with some new interpretation of the universe, nor is he presented as a moral teacher with a new moral code, though it is true that love is central to the way he presented his teaching, and this is echoed in the apostolic witness to Christ – not least in the presentation of Jesus in the Gospel of St John and in the letters of St Paul.

This sense that Jesus cannot be summed up in his teaching, whether philosophical or moral, is underlined by the fact that he wrote nothing himself; though this aligns him with another mysterious person, this time in the Greek tradition, Socrates. But in two ways Jesus gave his disciples something to remember him by. When the disciples asked him how to pray, he gave them the Lord's Prayer, the 'Our Father'; and on the night before he suffered, he asked his disciples to remember him by gathering together to break bread and share wine, receiving them as his body and blood.

This seems to me very significant for any attempt to develop a Christian understanding of God. Had Jesus presented himself as a philosopher, then we would naturally have looked to him for teaching on the nature of God and his relationship to the world, the nature of divine providence and so on. Had Jesus presented himself primarily as a moral teacher, then we would not be surprised if his notion of God turned on how God is a source of moral values, moral commandments and so on. And in the tradition of Western philosophy, going right back to Plato, we can see the way God has been invoked as the first cause, the ultimate explanation of everything, or as One who underwrites our moral values, either by issuing divine commandments for us to observe, or as himself the 'Form of the Good', or as the One who as Creator understands in a fundamental way human nature, so that from that understanding there can be derived a set of moral values, or a natural law.

All this might well be very important, and certainly a great deal of human thought has been devoted to understanding how God is the ultimate meaning of the universe or the ultimate source of moral values. But the ways Jesus wanted his disciples to remember him seem to me to suggest a different way of approaching the mystery of God. The Lord's Prayer first and foremost teaches us that God is the One to whom we pray; he is not some ultimate principle or final value, but one to whom we can address our prayers, one with whom we can enter into a relationship. We call him 'Father'; we are his children, his sons and daughters.

God as the One to whom we pray

The Lord's Prayer is said or sung at all the services of the Church. It has a central place in the divine liturgy: introducing the receiving of Holy Communion in the body and blood of Christ, and preceded by the eucharistic prayer, the anaphora ('offering' [prayer]), in which we address God, give thanks to him for all that he has given us 'known and unknown, manifest and hidden', recall his institution of the Holy Eucharist and call upon the Holy Spirit to come upon us and the gifts of bread and wine and transform them into the Holy body and blood of Christ, and then, in the very presence of Christ, beseech him for the Church and the world. It is the Church's prayer *par excellence*.

If God is the one to whom we pray, it is a natural question to ask: How do we speak about God in the central prayer of the divine liturgy? The longer of the two eucharistic prayers used regularly in the Orthodox Liturgy, the anaphora of St Basil, begins thus:

> Master, the One who is, Lord God, father Almighty, who are to be worshipped, it is truly right and fitting, and becomes the majesty of your holiness to praise you, to hymn you, to bless you, to worship you, to thank you, to glorify you, who alone are truly God; to offer you with a broken heart and a spirit of humility this our reasonable worship. For it is you who have granted us the knowledge of your truth. And who is able to tell of all your acts of power? To make all your praises heard or to recount all your wonders at every moment?
>
> Master of all things, Lord of heaven and earth and of all creation, seen and unseen, who are seated on a throne of glory and look upon the deeps, without beginning, invisible, unsearchable, uncircumscribed, unchangeable, the Father of our Lord, Jesus Christ, the great God and Saviour, our hope –
>
> who is the image of your goodness, perfect seal of your likeness, revealing you the Father in himself, living Word, true God, Wisdom before the ages, Life, Sanctification, Power, the true Light; through whom the Holy Spirit was made manifest –
>
> the Spirit of Truth, the grace of sonship, the pledge of the inheritance to come, the firstfruits of the eternal blessings, the life-giving power, the source of all sanctification –
>
> through whom every rational and intelligent creature is empowered, worships you and ascribes to you the everlasting hymn of glory, because all things are your servants. For Angels, Archangels, Thrones, Dominions, Principalities, Authorities, Powers, and the many-eyed Cherubim praise

18

you. Around you stand the Seraphim; the one has six wings and the other has six wings, and with two they cover their faces, with two their feet, and with two they fly, as they cry to one another with unceasing voices and never silent hymns of glory, singing, crying, shouting the triumphal hymn, and saying:

Holy, holy, holy, Lord of hosts; heaven and earth are full of your glory. Hosanna in the highest. Blessed is he who comes in the name of the Lord. Hosanna in the highest.[1]

We stand before God and address him in praise. We take on our lips the words and phrases of the Scriptures: from the initial words, expressing Jeremias' words of wonder (and recalling the whole context: 'The One who is, Master, Lord! Behold, I do not know how to speak . . .': Jer. 1.6), and going on to express the majesty and mystery of God, whom we know as the Father of our Lord Jesus Christ. The prayer then unfolds, using scriptural terminology, the mystery of the Trinity – in which the Father is manifest in the Son and the Spirit. The prayer continues, evoking Isaias' vision in the Temple (Isa. 6) of the worship of God by the angelic powers of heaven.

After joining our song with the song of the celestial power in the *Sanctus*, the prayer continues:

With these blessed Powers, O Master who love mankind, we sinners also cry aloud and say: Holy are you in truth, and All-holy, and there is no measure to the majesty of your holiness; and you are holy in all your works, because you have brought all things to pass for us with justice and true judgment. For you fashioned a man by taking dust from the earth, and honoured him, O God, with your own image. You placed him in the paradise of delight and promised him immortal life and the enjoyment of eternal blessings if he kept your commandments.[2]

We recall that it is through creation by God himself that we stand before God and are included in the prayer and praise of the powers of heaven.

. . . using the words he himself has given us

What this prayer teaches and exemplifies is that we stand before God, taking from his own revelation the words and phrases with which we address him. We address him as he has revealed himself – in

---

[1] Translation by Archimandrite Ephrem: *The Divine Liturgy of our Father among the Saints Basil the Great* (privately published, Manchester: St Andrew's Press, 2001), 27–8.
[2] *Liturgy of St Basil*, 28.

mystery and majesty, beyond any human conception – and also as Father, Son and Holy Spirit, again expressed in words and phrases drawn from the Scriptures themselves. What the Scriptures have given us is a way of addressing God, a way that matches something of the glory of his nature, but not a way of defining him.

It is something like this that St Maximos the Confessor develops in his short treatise on the *Our Father*. The petitions of the Lord's Prayer constitute a theology, but it is theology of a particular sort. As Maximos puts it:

> For hidden within a limited compass this prayer contains the whole purpose and aim of which we have just spoken [viz., the divine counsel whose purpose is the deification of our nature]; . . . The prayer includes petitions for everything that the divine Word effected through his self-emptying in the Incarnation, and it teaches us to strive for those blessings of which the true provider is God the Father alone through the natural mediation of the Son in the Holy Spirit . . .

Maximos goes on to discuss the seven mysteries contained in the prayer: 'theology, adoption of sons by grace, equality with the angels, participation in eternal life, the restoration of human nature . . . , the abolition of the law of sin, and the destruction of the tyranny . . . of the evil one'. These are not just mysteries to contemplate, still less to solve; they are mysteries that draw us into communion with God. They reveal the mystery of the Trinity (which is what Maximos means by 'theology', *theologia*), and that this opens up to us the possibility of adoption as sons and daughters in the Son, Christ. This state of adoption grants us equality with the angels ('on earth, as in heaven'). We participate in the divine life through making Christ himself our food, pre-eminently in the Holy Eucharist. Human nature is restored to itself; for human kind has been fragmented by the Fall, we are separated from one another, opposed to each other – restoration takes place through forgiveness ('Forgive us our debts, as we forgive our debtors'). But life on earth remains a constant struggle against evil; we recognize this as we pray for deliverance from temptation. And we seek deliverance from the power of the evil one.[3]

---

[3] The passage summarized can be found in Maximos the Confessor, *On the Lord's Prayer*, in *Opuscula exegetica duo* (ed. P. Van Deun; CCSG, 23; Turnhout: Brepols, 1991), 62–176 (Eng. trans. slightly modified, in *The Philokalia: The Complete Text*; vol. 2 [trans. G. E. H. Palmer, Philip Sherrard and Kallistos Ware; London and Boston: Faber & Faber, 1981], 286–90).

Because these mysteries are about our transformation into God, deification, they are presented to us in the Lord's Prayer as petitions, expressions of our desire, or perhaps better, to use a phrase of Thomas Aquinas, as interpreting our desire: *desiderii interpres*.[4] Maximos sees this desire as a response to God's love for us, in particular, God's love for us manifest in the Incarnation and self-emptying of the Son of God, and a response that demands of us a similar self-emptying: '[m]oreover, by emptying themselves of the passions they lay hold of the divine to the same degree as that to which, deliberately emptying Himself of his own sublime glory, the Word of God truly became man'.[5]

If we turn to God in prayer, we expect him to listen, to hear our prayers. What we might mean by that is a mystery – and mystery, in the sense not of a puzzle to solve but something of which we have some understanding, but an even deeper sense that such understanding will never be exhaustive, there will always be more to say, is something we shall encounter throughout this book. But it at least means that we can be attentive to God and expect his attention to us. In some way, prayer opens up a personal relationship; prayer is an activity only open to persons (except metaphorically), and can only be addressed to a person. So, if we think of God as one to whom we pray, we are thinking of God in personal terms. I have put it like that, rather than saying 'as a person', for two reasons. First of all, the notion of a person is quite a slippery notion, as we shall discover later on when we think what we mean by saying that human beings are persons created 'in God's image'. Second, do we Christians think of God as 'a' person? Don't we in fact think of God as a Trinity of Persons, Father, Son and Holy Spirit? How did Christians come by the notion of the Trinity? And what does it mean?

God as Trinity

The word 'trinity', from the Latin *trinitas*, means a set of three, not a random set of three, but three things that in some way belong together. *Trinitas* is the Latin equivalent of the Greek *trias*. Despite appearances, there is really no suggestion in the Latin word that it

---

[4] Thomas Aquinas, *Summa Theologiae* IIaIIae. 83. 1 ad 1.
[5] Maximos, *On the Lord's Prayer*, in *Opuscula exegetica duo*, 102–6 (*Philokalia*, 287).

means a kind of threefold unity, a tri-unity, so I do not think, as Orthodox, we need abandon the words 'Trinity' and 'trinitarian' for the Greek-based 'Triad' and 'triadological', as some do.

The word itself, *trias*, does not occur in the New Testament; it first emerges in the second century in the Christian apologist, Theophilos of Antioch. But the set of three to which the Trinity refers is frequent in the New Testament, for the set of three is Father, Son and Holy Spirit. God the Son is the Lord Jesus Christ, who prays to God as his Father; the Holy Spirit is a mysterious presence of God, experienced in the Christian Church. There is, and remains in Greek theology in particular, a sense that 'God' is the Father; a common expression in Greek theology in the fourth and fifth centuries, and indeed later, speaks of *ho Theos kai Pater*, 'the God and Father', often translated, rather lazily, as 'God the Father'. So there is a very strong sense in the New Testament and in later Greek theology that 'God', *ho Theos*, refers to the Father. This usage makes clear that the monotheism of the Hebrews is something affirmed, not qualified, by the Christian faith. What happened – very quickly, within decades of the crucifixion of Christ – is that Christ is seen as ranked with the God and Father as God, and (perhaps less clearly) the Holy Spirit, too.

How did the Church move from the Hebrew monotheism of the early disciples of Christ to the Trinitarian theology that has come to define Christianity? In one way, this is a long and complex story that we cannot tell here;[6] but in another way it is a very simple story, indeed hardly a story at all, rather a realization we can trace in the earliest documents of the Christian faith. In fact, the long and complex story might rather be regarded as an account of the efforts by the Church to avoid a series of misunderstandings of a faith expressed primarily in worship and prayer, but easily misconceived in concepts and philosophical categories. We may touch on the 'long and complex story' at times in this book, but here let us look at the simple realization.

There are several events in the Gospels where the Trinitarian nature of God is revealed: examples are the baptism of Christ, the

---

[6] For a fine account of this story by an Orthodox scholar, see John Behr, *The Way to Nicaea* (Crestwood, NY: St Vladimir's Seminary Press, 2001) and *The Nicene Faith*, parts 1 and 2 (Crestwood, NY: St Vladimir's Seminary Press, 2004). For a much briefer account, see my *St John Damascene: Tradition and Originality in Byzantine Theology* (Oxford: Oxford University Press, 2002), 95–100.

Transfiguration, and the agony in the garden. At Christ's baptism, as the Lord ascends from the waters, the heavens open, the Spirit of God descends on him in the form of a dove and there is heard the voice of the Father saying, 'You are my beloved Son, in whom I am well pleased' (or in the Lucan version: 'You are my Son, today I have begotten you'). The Orthodox Church celebrates the baptism of Christ on the Feast of the Theophany, the 'manifestation of God'. In the icon of the baptism, or Theophany, the Trinity is intimated in the man, the dove and the Father's blessing. The apolytikion of the feast expresses its meaning in these words:

> As you were baptized in the Jordan, Lord, the worship of the Trinity was made manifest, for the voice of the Father bore witness to you, naming you the Beloved Son; and the Spirit, in the form of a dove, confirmed the sureness of the word. Christ our God, who appeared and enlightened the world, glory to you.[7]

Notice that it is the *worship* of the Trinity that is made manifest at this feast, not the doctrine; as we contemplate the mystery of Christ's baptism we are drawn to worship the Holy Trinity, who enlightens the world through the Incarnate Son.

At the Transfiguration, Christ appeared to the inner three of the disciples – Peter, James and John – transfigured in his glory and accompanied by the prophets Moses and Elias. Again there is a voice from heaven, the voice of the Father saying, 'This is my Beloved Son'; again the Spirit appears, this time in the form of the cloud that descends on the scene, from which the voice is heard – the cloud of the divine presence, the *Shekinah*, that filled the tabernacle in the Old Testament. This time, however, what is manifest is principally that the Son belongs to the Holy Trinity, and therefore that it is as God that Christ is going to his voluntary passion: on the cross, 'one of the Trinity suffered in the flesh', in a phrase that became popular from the fifth century onwards. The kontakion of the feast interprets its meaning in these words:

> You were transfigured on the mountain, and your Disciples beheld your glory, Christ our God, as far as they were able; that when they saw you crucified, they might know that your suffering was voluntary,

---

[7] *An Orthodox Prayer Book* (Eng. trans. Archimandrite Ephrem Lash; Milton under Wychwood: St Alban & St Sergius, 2009), 102.

and might proclaim to the world that you are truly the brightness of the Father.[8]

Throughout Holy Week, it is made clear that Christ's suffering was voluntary; in the anaphora of St John Chrysostom this is expressed by referring to 'the night in which he was given up, *or rather gave himself up*, for the life of the world'.[9] And this is made clear in the mystery of the Garden of Gethsemane, where Christ withdrew with the inner three of the disciples to pray to the Father. To his disciples, he says, 'my soul is greatly troubled, even unto death'; to his Father, he prays, 'My Father, if it be possible, let this cup pass from me; nevertheless, not as I will, but as you' (Matt. 26.38–39). St Luke records that 'being in agony he prayed still more intensely; and his sweat became as drops of blood falling on the earth' (Luke 22.44).

Prayer and the Trinity

It is here, I think, that we see most clearly what it was that compelled Christians to think of the One God in terms of the Holy Trinity. For in the Garden of Gethsemane, the Father and the Son are clearly distinct. Metropolitan Philaret spoke of 'The love of the Father crucifying, the love of the Son crucified, and the love of the Holy Spirit triumphant in the invincible power of the cross'.[10] All three persons of the Trinity are involved in the crucifixion as an act of redeeming love, but they are clearly distinct. And that distinction, as the prayer in Gethsemane makes clear, is articulated *through prayer*. It is the Son's prayer to the Father that makes clear the distinction – the *personal* distinction – between the Father and the Son.

But there is a dual character to the Son's prayer to the Father, for the Son prays to the Father both as God the Son and as the Incarnate Son: his prayer allows us to glimpse something of the nature both of the relationship within the Divine Trinity as Christ prays to the Father as his Son, and of his relationship to us as Christ prays to God

---

[8] *Orthodox Prayer Book*, 104.

[9] *The Divine Liturgy of our Father among the Saints John Chrysostom* (Oxford: Oxford University Press, 1995), 32 (my italics).

[10] Quoted by Vladimir Lossky in his *The Mystical Theology of the Eastern Church* (London: James Clarke & Co., 1957), 85.

the Father, as the Son, the 'firstborn among many brethren' (Rom. 8.29). There is one person praying – the Incarnate Son of God (there is no separate human person; we shall see more of this later on) – but his prayer expresses a dual filial relationship: the relationship of the Son to the Father within the Trinity and the relationship of the human sonship that God the Son assumed in the Incarnation, a relationship into which we are incorporated by the adoption as sons and daughters that is effected in baptism, so that we are counted 'worthy . . . with boldness and without condemnation to dare to call upon the God of heaven, as Father, and to say: Our Father . . .'.[11]

We can see something of this duality in the Gospels. All the Gospels refer to Jesus' prayer to his Father; Jesus is depicted as spending whole nights alone in prayer to God who is his Father. These accounts inspire us to devote ourselves seriously to prayer. But there are other passages where Christ is, as it were, assimilated to God; we are not so much expected to enter into his prayer, as to pray to him, to find in Jesus the Lord the source of succour and salvation. An example is the passage in St Matthew's Gospel, where the Lord says: 'Come to me, all that labour and are heavy laden, and I will give you rest. Take my yoke upon you and learn of me; for I am meek and lowly in heart: and you shall find rest for your souls' (Matt. 11.28–29). This sense of the Incarnate Son as sent by the Father and turning to the Father in prayer is the fundamental *Leitmotif* of St John's Gospel.

The Holy Spirit

This realization of the dual aspect of Christ – leading us in prayer to God, and also being the One to whom we pray, 'one of the Trinity' – is something we shall explore later on when we come to consider who Christ is: what is called 'Christology'. Here we are interested in the other side of this: the way in which a relationship within the Godhead between Father and Son, articulated in prayer, brought about a realization of God as Trinity.

You might say that what I have just said only makes clear a relationship between the Father and the Son: What about the Holy Spirit?

---

[11] Priest's invitation to the people to join in the Lord's Prayer in the divine liturgy: cf. *Liturgy of St John Chrysostom*, 39.

It was, indeed, popular among Western scholars in the last century or so to maintain that in the development of the doctrine of the Trinity there was a 'binitarian' stage, a stage of the 'two-in-oneness' of the Father and the Son in the Godhead. Such a view seems much less popular nowadays, and indeed it seems to me to be based on a false model of doctrinal 'development', as if the doctrine of the Trinity is really 'later' than the New Testament and the revelation of Christ. Rather, I have spoken in terms of 'realization': the realization that the One Godhead embraced persons in relationship, a realization that may have taken centuries to articulate in the language that the Church later regarded as canonical; nevertheless that realization seems to me aboriginal.

But what about the Holy Spirit? The language about the Holy Spirit in the Scriptures is much less straightforward; sometimes it seems to be a matter of someone personal, but on other occasions the language seems more general, referring to the divine presence or activity. First, however, we must make one thing clear. What I have outlined above is not, in any sense, a *proof* of the relationship between Father and Son in the Trinity; certainly not in the sense of explaining *why* there are Father and Son in the Trinity. It is a point frequently made by the Fathers that we cannot answer the question 'Why?' in relation to the Godhead; only in matters concerning the created order can we hope to answer this question, and not always then. All we can hope to do is catch some glimpse of the mystery of the Holy Trinity, but we shall never understand it. The case of the Holy Spirit may well be more mysterious; it does not make it less important, as we shall see later.

There are, however, some things we can say even now. First, as Fathers, such as St Athanasios and St Basil, pointed out when the divinity of the Holy Spirit was called in question in the fourth century, the role of the Spirit is to effect the presence of the Holy Spirit in those who believe: deification takes place through the Spirit, all the sacraments involve the descent of the Holy Spirit in power. None of this would make sense if the Holy Spirit did not belong to the Holy Trinity. Furthermore, the Holy Spirit comes in answer to prayer, to his being invoked, which would only make sense if he, too, were personal. And, perhaps most significant, the Holy Spirit is invoked in Christian worship alongside the Father and the Son: baptism is in the name of the Father, Son and Holy Spirit. Christian worship is addressed to the Father, through the Son, and in the Holy Spirit – or, more briefly, to the Father, the Son and the Holy Spirit. 'Glory to the Father, and to the Son, and to the Holy Spirit' is one of the most frequent phrases in Christian worship, both in the West and the East. It is in what appear to be liturgical passages, preserved in the early writings of the Church, including the New Testament, that we find the most consistent witness to the Trinity; the earliest Christian hymn we know – 'Gladdening Light', *Phos hilaron* – is Trinitarian in both structure and meaning.

The dogma of the Trinity

Gradually the Church developed a terminology in which to express her understanding of God the Holy Trinity, one God in three persons. In order to achieve clarity, the Church came to adopt a technical language. We need to be clear about what kind of clarity was sought. At no point did the Church seek to solve the mystery of the Trinity: that was an accusation often made, whether justly or not, against the heretics, the proponents of positions rejected by the Church. We speak of 'definitions' of the faith, most notably, in relation to Christology, of the 'Chalcedonian Definition' issued by the Œcumenical Council in 451. 'Definition', in English, suggests some precise description, an account of what something really is. But the etymological origins of the word rather suggest establishing a boundary (Latin: *finis*); indeed, the Greek word used by the Council – *horos* – simply means 'a boundary'. The Chalcedonian 'Definition', then, should be understood not as defining precisely how Christ is both God and man and yet one, but rather laying down a boundary, beyond which is heresy. For, although the mysteries of the faith are beyond understanding, they are not beyond *mis*understanding, and the conciliar definitions are intended to prevent such misunderstanding.

The first technical term to be introduced was the word, *homoousios*, 'consubstantial': it was affirmed of the Son in the creed of the Council of Nicaea, the First Œcumenical Council (AD 325), that he is *homoousios*, consubstantial, with the Father, meaning that he derives his very being from the Father and is equal to him, not some sort of subordinate. Later in the century, it was made clear that the Holy Spirit, too, is consubstantial with the Father. This entailed the assertion that there was only one divine substance or essence, or *ousia*: and that this expresses the unity of the Godhead.

But the divine *ousia* or essence was not to be understood – as with other generic terms – as what it is to be divine; that would not have safeguarded the unity of God, just as one human nature does not mean that there is only one man. Rather the divine *ousia* was understood to be the Father's being – the being of the one God we call Father – which has been extended in unbroken continuity to the Son, through begetting, and to the Holy Spirit, through procession. This was expressed in the amplified version of the Creed of Nicaea, issued in connexion with the Second Œcumenical Council of Constantinople (held in 381), which defined the orthodox religion of the Emperor Theodosios' Christian Roman Empire (this version of the creed is often referred to as the 'Nicene Creed', and is the form of the creed used by both the Eastern and Western Churches in worship, especially in the eucharistic liturgy – except by the Armenians, who use the actual creed of 325).

By this time further terminology was developing (not stated explicitly in the Nicene Creed): God exists as three persons in one substance or essence. The preferred term for 'person' in Greek was not *prosopon*, though this word was used, but *hypostasis*, a word that could mean 'being', and is an exact equivalent ('calque') of the Latin *substantia*, 'substance'; so that the Greeks spoke of one *ousia* and three *hypostases*. The Latins, on the other hand, used their traditional terminology that can be traced back to Tertullian in the early third century, of one *substantia* and three *personae* – one substance and three persons. It is easy to see that this terminology might lead to confusion as Latins and Greeks spoke to one another. But that is not our concern now.

The affirmation of One God existing in three co-equal persons leads naturally to the notion of the Trinity – *trinitas, trias* – and we begin to find the Christian God thought of simply as the Trinity. In the early fifth century, we find works called *On the Trinity*: both Cyril of Alexandria and Augustine of Hippo wrote works with such a title. Alongside prayer to the Father, through the Son, and in the Holy Spirit – the form of prayer found in many liturgies, out of which emerged the realization of the mystery of the Trinity – we find devotion directed specifically to the Trinity, for instance in St Gregory the Theologian's poem, 'On his Life', which ends with the prayer:

I pray that it [my life] will end up in the unshakeable home
Where lives the bright union of my Trinity,
By whose faint reflection we are now raised up.[12]

The note of personal devotion is manifest in his reference to 'my Trinity'.

In Augustine's *De Trinitate*, we can, I think, see the beginnings of a concern for what one might call the 'mystery of the Trinity'; in Cyril's *On the Holy Trinity*, we find something much more traditional – a sense of God the Father revealed through the Son and the Holy Spirit, both consubstantial with the Father.

The Trinity and the apophatic

This traditional approach is found in what is perhaps the most developed expression of Greek theology: the first eight chapters of *On the Orthodox Faith* by the eighth-century theologian, St John Damascene.[13] This begins with an assertion of the incomprehensibility of God: for all the technical language John is going to introduce, it remains axiomatic for John that here we are approaching a mystery that is beyond human comprehension. It is not, however, as if God kept the mysteries of his being in some kind of jealous possessiveness; rather, God wants to make himself known, he longs to share his being and life with his creatures. Only in that coming to know the uncreated God, we shall be overwhelmed by the mystery of his being, the inexhaustibility of any knowledge we may glimpse of him.

John goes on to outline various ways in which the sense of the mystery of God has been preserved in Christian theology. First and foremost, we cannot know God, only what he is not – not-finite, not-created, not-visible – something expressed in Greek by the alpha-privative, so that we have almost a theology of the alpha-privative, for instance, at the beginning of the anaphora of St John Chrysostom, where God is confessed as *anekphrastos, aperinoetos, aoratos, akataleptos* – ineffable, incomprehensible, invisible, inconceivable. Furthermore,

---

[12] 'Concerning his own life', lines 1947–9, in Gregory of Nazianzus, *Autobiographical Poems* (ed. and trans. Carolinne White; Cambridge Medieval Classics, 6; Cambridge: Cambridge University Press, 1996), 152–3.

[13] For more detail, see my *St John Damascene*, 89–116.

we do not know God, we only know 'about' him; we do not know his being or essence, only his activity, *energeia*, or power.

John also evokes a distinction between *theologia* and *oikonomia* – theology and the economy – God in himself, essentially the Trinity, and God in his dealings with the created order; we know the latter much better than the former, though even in the economy much is beyond our understanding. He refers, as well, to the distinction, introduced into Christian theology by one we call 'Dionysios the Areopagite', between kataphatic and apophatic theology – theology of affirmation (Greek: *kataphasis*), in which we affirm what God has revealed of himself, and theology of negation (*apophasis*), in which we deny that our concepts match up to the reality of God; apophatic theology being more fundamental.

Having thus made clear the indirectness of our language about God, John Damascene introduces us to the notion of God as One, and underlines the reality of the One God confessed in the Scriptures in contrast with the many gods of pagan polytheism (in making so much of this, John may have had in mind his Muslim contemporaries and political masters, for he was writing in Palestine after the Arab conquest of the seventh century). This one God, however, manifests himself as Word and Spirit, which flow from the Father, and are one with him: it is through the Word and the Spirit that we come to know God, the Father.

Coinherence and love in the Trinity

We then come to a long chapter, 'On the holy Triad', in which John explores what we can make of the holy Trinity. Again, he starts by emphasizing that this is all beyond our comprehension, all we can hope for is to avoid misunderstanding that will lead us away from God rather than open our hearts to him. He introduces the language we have already mentioned: the one *ousia* of God, the three *hypostases* of the Trinity. But he also introduces a concept that had not hitherto been used with much confidence in relation to the Holy Trinity: the idea of *perichoresis*, 'interpenetration' or 'coinherence'. The persons of the Trinity are not separate from each other, as human persons are, rather they interpenetrate one another. Without losing their distinctness as persons, their reality coincides or coinheres. John is quite clear, in contrast to some modern Orthodox theologians, that what is the case with the Trinity is *not* the case with human beings; the Trinitarian communion of persons is not a model for human communion. Rather, it is characteristic of the *uncreated* nature of the Godhead that the persons should coinhere with one another; with created natures it is different – in reality they are separate; any communion they have is a form of sharing.

It seems to me that the doctrine of *perichoresis*, coinherence, that John introduces into Christian theology, expresses well the realization that within the Trinity there is relationship, a relationship expressed in prayer. There is, as it were, a kind of mutual yielding within the Trinity: the Father makes space for the Son and the Spirit (to use obviously inappropriate, spatial language), and the Son and the Spirit yield to the Father as they turn to him in prayer. This is expressed, in the rare economy of paint, in the Trinity Icon of St Andrey Rublev: the mutual gestures of the Father (on the left, as you face it), the Son who becomes incarnate (in the middle) and the Holy Spirit (on the right), are gestures of mutual respect, yielding and therefore affirmation.[14]

There is a beautiful passage in a short treatise by Clement of Alexandria, *Who is the rich man who is being saved?*, which was composed perhaps at the end of the second century:

> Behold the mysteries of love, and then you will have a vision of the bosom of the Father, whom the only-begotten God alone declared. God in His very self is love, and for love's sake He became visible to us. And while in his ineffability He is Father, in his sympathy with us he has become Mother. By his loving the Father became feminine, a great sign of which is the one he begat from himself; and the fruit born of love is love. For this reason he came down, for this reason he put on human nature, for this reason he willingly suffered what belongs to being human, so that having been measured to the weakness of those he loved, he might in return measure us to his own power.[15]

It flows from love's very self, Clement is saying, that the Son became human in the Incarnation. His self-emptying (measuring himself to

---

[14] On this see (now Archimandrite) Gabriel Bunge, *The Rublev Trinity* (Crestwood, NY: St Vladimir's Seminary Press, 2007), esp. 89–99.

[15] Clement of Alexandria, *Quis dives salvetur* 37 (cf. *Clement of Alexandria* [trans. G. W. Butterworth; Loeb Classical Library; London: Heinemann, 1919]; the translation here, however, is mine).

our weakness) expresses his very being: the love that reveals that he belongs to the Father's bosom. In emptying himself, the Son does not become something else, he simply expresses himself, expresses what he is: love from love.

The fundamental nature of the apophatic

As we follow this through, I think we can begin to grasp the deeper meaning of the stress on the apophatic, on incomprehension in the face of the mystery of God, that we have already encountered in this book, and that might almost be regarded as the signature tune of Orthodox theology of the twentieth century. For apophatic theology is not about some higher way with concepts, some ultimate refinement of a human conceptual theology – kataphatic theology and apophatic theology being deployed as we handle our concepts of God like the tacking a pilot uses in sailing a boat. To say that apophatic theology is fundamental is to say something rather different, something expressed in a telling way by Vladimir Lossky towards the end of his great work, *The Mystical Theology of the Eastern Church*:

> We have had again and again, in the course of our study of the mystical theology of the Eastern Church, to refer to the apophatic attitude which is characteristic of its religious thought. As we have seen, the negations which draw attention to the divine incomprehensibility are not prohibitions upon knowledge: apophaticism, so far from being a limitation, enables us to transcend all concepts, every sphere of philosophical speculation. It is a tendency towards an ever-greater plenitude, in which knowledge is transformed into ignorance, the theology of concepts into contemplation, dogmas into experience of ineffable mysteries. It is, moreover, an existential theology involving man's entire being, which sets him upon the way of union, which obliges him to be changed, to transform his nature that he may attain to the true *gnosis* which is the contemplation of the Holy Trinity. Now, this 'change of heart', this *metanoia*, means repentance. The apophatic way of Eastern theology is the repentance of the human person before the face of the living God.[16]

---

[16] Lossky, *The Mystical Theology of the Eastern Church*, 238.

3

The doctrine of creation

The anaphora of St John Chrysostom begins like this:

> It is right and fitting to hymn you, to bless you, to praise you, to give you thanks, to worship you in every place of your dominion; for you are God, ineffable, incomprehensible, invisible, inconceivable, ever existing, eternally the same; you and your only-begotten Son and your Holy Spirit. You brought us out of non-existence into being, and when we had fallen you raised us up again, and left nothing undone until you had brought us up to heaven and had granted us your kingdom that is to come.
>
> For all these things we give thanks to you, and to your only-begotten Son and your Holy Spirit; for all the benefits that we have received, known and unknown, manifest and hidden.[1]

The prayer begins by addressing God who exists beyond being and knowledge and who calls us into being, in order to care for us and bring us to communion with him in heaven and the kingdom that is to come. This care is displayed in his showering on us benefits, both those we are aware of and those beyond our understanding. We stand before God in prayer, because he created us and cares for us. The God we address in this prayer is the God we have already confessed in the creed, read or sung immediately before the beginning of the eucharistic prayer: 'One God, Father almighty, Maker of heaven and earth, and of all things visible and invisible'. The spelling out of what has been made, or created – heaven and earth, all things visible and invisible – is partly to underline the fact that God created everything; there is nothing that exists that he did not create, apart from the Holy Trinity, which is consubstantial, *homoousios*, with God the Father. But the mention of heaven and things invisible reminds us that the created order is not limited to the world of visible earthly beings; we shall have more to say of that later.

---

[1] *The Divine Liturgy of our Father among the Saints John Chrysostom* (Oxford: Oxford University Press, 1995), 31.

The prominence of the doctrine of creation is further underlined by the fact that the very first book of the Bible, Genesis, begins with an account of the creation of the world in six days (Gen. 1.1—2.3), followed by a more discursive account of the creation of human kind, Adam and Eve (Gen. 2.4–24). This emphasis on creation is even more evident in the Greek Septuagint translation, which calls this first book *Genesis* (or in some manuscripts: *Genesis Kosmou*): 'The coming-into-being [of the world]', in contrast to the Hebrew, which simply calls the book by its first word, *B^{e}rêshith*, 'In the beginning'. In the first few Christian centuries, commentaries on the first chapter of Genesis, sometimes spilling over into the second chapter, were very common – Eusebios in his *Church History* lists eight; they were generally referred to as commentaries on the *Hexaemeron*, 'Six Days'. It was a tradition inherited from the Jews: Philo's treatise *On the Making of the World* had a great influence on subsequent Christian exegesis. The most famous and influential Greek commentary was the *Hexaemeron* by St Basil the Great, an incomplete set of homilies, which did not get to treating the creation of human kind, an omission made good by his younger brother, St Gregory of Nyssa, in his short treatise, *On the Making of Human kind*.[2]

The early Christian doctrine of creation

It is clear from this that the doctrine of creation was immensely important for early Christians. The reason for this is not far to seek, for the doctrine of creation was not a generally held belief, except among Jews and Christians, in late antiquity, and for them it conveyed something very important.

The idea of the origin of the world was a matter about which human beings had long speculated. Ancient myths had told of the emergence of the earth as a result of some struggle among the gods; Hesiod in his *Theogony* told of the emergence of earth in the context of the genealogy of the gods. Perhaps the most influential account of the origin of the cosmos in the intellectual world that the early Christians inhabited – also called a myth – was that given in Plato's

---

[2] For more detail on this, see my 'The Fathers on Genesis', in *The Book of Genesis: Composition, Reception, and Interpretation* (ed. Craig A. Evans, Joel N. Lohr and David L. Petersen; Leiden: Brill, 2012), 561–78.

Timaeus. But these are accounts – either mythological or in terms of ancient science – intended to explain features of the world, how it all fits together. They are, very broadly speaking, concerned with the bringing of order out of chaos and darkness, and there are traces of this in the Genesis account which seems to speak of darkness and the abyss as the context or matrix in which God created heaven and earth ('The earth was unseen and unformed, and there was darkness over the abyss', Gen. 1.2a, LXX).

But many Christians, like Jews such as Philo, read the Genesis account as telling of a radical *creation* of the cosmos, not just the introduction of order to a formless, abysmal darkness. Round about the time of Christ, we begin to find emerging a more precise notion of creation as creation out of nothing – *ex ouk onton, ex nihilo*. The first mention of this in the biblical books occurs in 2 Maccabees, in the account of the martyrdom of the seven Maccabaean martyrs at the hands of the Seleucid king, Antiochos IV Epiphanes. Antiochos had tortured and killed six of the sons of their devout mother, by tradition called Salomina, and appealed to her to plead with her youngest son to eat pork, thus breaking the Law and saving his life. Instead, in Hebrew, which further infuriated Antiochos, she supported her son's resolve:

> My son, have pity on me. I carried you nine months in my womb . . . I beseech you, my child, to look at the heaven and the earth and see everything that is in them, and recognize that God did not make them out of things that exist (*ouk ex onton epoiesen ho theos*). Do not fear this butcher, but prove worthy of your brothers. Accept death, so that in God's mercy I may get you back again with your brothers.
>
> (2 Macc. 7.27–29)

It is an enormously moving scene, but it is more than that. In making this first explicit confession of the doctrine of creation out of nothing, Salomina appeals to this doctrine to seal the martyrdom of her son, and to justify the doctrine of the resurrection, in which she is confident she will receive him back with his brothers. It is striking that it is in precisely the same context – of martyrdom and the conviction of the resurrection – that we find Christians in the second century becoming more and more confident that what they believe about creation is that it is created out of nothing by God.

So we find a belief in creation, not in the sense of simply bringing order out of chaos, but in the more radical sense that God created the cosmos out of nothing, 'not out of the things that are', as Salomina put it. Since it was such a radical belief, and, we may presume, because it is rarely affirmed explicitly in the Bible – 2 Maccabees 7.28 is the only clear text; when Christians later try to marshal biblical texts in support of the doctrine of creation, they are hard put to find them[3] – for both these reasons the explicit doctrine of creation out of nothing developed slowly. Justin Martyr still seems to accept the Platonic doctrine that God created the cosmos out of pre-existent matter;[4] Origen's belief in creation out of nothing only seems to extend to the material creation.[5] Theophilos, in the second century, is perhaps the first to affirm creation out of nothing,[6] and by the beginning of the fourth century, the doctrine is firmly established among Christians, as St Athanasios' treatise *On the Incarnation* makes clear.[7] Nonetheless, the difficulty in conceptualizing such a radical belief does not detract from the fact that the fundamental intuition behind it – a conviction that there is nothing that falls outside the power of God – is firmly rooted in the Scriptures.

Creation out of nothing

As Christians reflected on the doctrine of creation out of nothing by God, they found that the doctrine came to form what the early twentieth-century Russian philosopher and theologian, Fr Pavel Florensky, called an antinomy, that is two assertions opposed to each other, even contradicting each other, both of which have to be affirmed.[8] On the one hand, the doctrine of creation spoke of an absolute difference between God and all things created; there is nothing in common between the being of God the Holy Trinity and the being of created entities. On the other hand, the doctrine of creation meant that the creature – each creature – owes everything

---

[3] Origen, appealing to scriptural authority for creation out of nothing, quotes, beside 2 Maccabees 7.28, from the *Shepherd of Hermas* (*Mand.* I. 1), and from Psalm 148.5 ('he spoke, and it was made').
[4] Justin Martyr, *Apologia* I. 59.
[5] Origen, *De Principiis* II. 1. 4–5.
[6] Theophilos, *Ad Autolycum* II. 10.
[7] Athanasios, *De Incarnatione* 3, quoting *Mand.* I. 1 from the *Shepherd of Hermas*, Genesis 1.1 and Hebrews 11.3.
[8] See Pavel Florensky, *The Pillar and Ground of the Truth* (trans. Boris Jakim; Princeton, NJ: Princeton University Press, 1997), 114–23.

that it is to the Creator; there is nothing in being created that is intrinsically opposed to the Creator. Let us take each side of the antinomy separately.

The notion of an absolute difference between God and creation cut at the root of one of the convictions of what has been called the cosmic piety of late antiquity, which drew on both Platonic and Stoic notions. Both these strains of philosophical thought envisaged a world of gods and men – immortals and mortals – in which, though there was a difference, it was not absolute; in all sorts of ways the boundary between the divine and the human was porous – it could be breached. The realm of the gods was what humans could aspire to.

Within Platonism, the distinction was seen more precisely as being between the realms of the spiritual and the material, of which Socrates had said, in the *Phaedo*,

> On the one hand we have that which is divine, immortal, indestructible, of a single form, accessible to thought, ever constant and abiding true to itself; and the soul is very like it: on the other hand we have that which is human, mortal, destructible, of many forms, inaccessible to thought, never constant nor abiding true to itself; and the body is very like that.[9]

A spiritual, immaterial world, where the soul belongs – and a material world, where the body belongs: the ultimate purpose of the soul is to detach itself from the material world of the bodily and return to the spiritual world, to realize its kinship with that world. As Plato put it in a much later dialogue, the *Theaetetus*, 'flight [from the world] is assimilation to God as far as this is possible'.[10]

This vision of the soul's ascent to God had been, and was to remain, very attractive to many Christians; for Clement of Alexandria, writing at the turn of the third century, the quotation above from the *Theaetetus* was one of his favourites. But the doctrine of creation out of nothing posed problems, for it suggested that the fundamental division within reality was not between the spiritual and the material, but between the created and the uncreated. Indeed, more radically even than that, it suggested that the divide between God and creation was not a divide within any encompassing 'reality', but a distinction

---

[9] Plato, *Phaedo* 80B; R. Hackforth's translation in *Plato's Phaedo* (Cambridge: Cambridge University Press, 1972), 84.
[10] Plato, *Theaetetus* 176B.

between two kinds of being that were incommensurate with each other, so that if one is called real, the other must be called unreal, and vice versa. As St Gregory Palamas put it, in the fourteenth century, '[God] is not a being, if the others are beings; and if he is a being, the others are not beings'.[11] There can be no idea that the soul is 'really' divine, and finds its true being in union with God; that ascent to God is a kind of 'homecoming' as the soul returns whence it has come, abandoning the body, which has a different origin, for soul and body share a single origin in the creative will of God.

This leads, first of all and notably, in St Gregory of Nyssa, to the notion that, as the soul draws nearer and nearer to God, it doesn't find itself on 'home territory', so to speak; rather, in drawing closer and closer to a God who is utterly different from it, it realizes more and more poignantly that God is utterly unknowable. Gregory expresses this in his treatise *The Life of Moses*, where he sees the life of the soul reflected in the progress of Moses' life, from his first encounter with God in the light of the burning bush, leading up Mount Sinai through the clouds and darkness, into the impenetrable cloud at the summit of the mountain, where he finds, not God himself, but the place where God dwells. It is a progress from light to darkness, from understanding to a trust in the sense of presence that he cannot grasp or make complete sense of. For Gregory the contrast between created being and the uncreated God is a contrast between what we can know – in accordance with the epistemological principle that 'like knows like' – and what is beyond our knowledge, between the finite, that we are familiar with, and the infinite, which is beyond anything we can grasp.[12]

The other side of the antinomy is that everything in the creature is from God, that there is nothing in the creature opposed to God. The creaturely experience of this is twofold, even antinomic. On the one hand, everything we are is good, 'exceedingly good', coming from the hand of the Creator; there is nothing at the level of being that is opposed to God, no irreducible evil in the created order. If we

---

[11] Gregory Palamas, *One Hundred and Fifty Chapters* 78 (ed. and trans. Robert E. Sinkewicz; Studies and Texts 83; Toronto: Pontifical Institute of Mediaeval Studies, 1988, 173).

[12] For a good introduction to this aspect of Gregory of Nyssa's theology, with a selection of texts in translation, see *From Glory to Glory: Texts from Gregory of Nyssa* (selected and introduced by Jean Daniélou; trans. and ed. Herbert Musurillo; London: John Murray, 1962).

follow the grain of our being, as it were, we shall find ourselves in harmony with God. On the other hand, we bring nothing of our own to our being; we are 'out of nothing', our very nature is 'once not to have existed', as St Athanasios put it.[13]

This 'nothing', from which we have come through God's creative act, is the only place to which we can turn, if we choose to turn away from the God who gave us being: this provides the dynamics of the doctrine of the Fall, to which we shall turn in another chapter. But the point now is rather different. The fundamental antinomy of Creation can be expressed in a vivid image from a sermon by St Philaret, the great Metropolitan of Moscow in the nineteenth century, who said that 'the creative Word is like an adamantine bridge, upon which creatures stand balanced beneath the abyss of divine infinitude, and above that of their own nothingness'.[14] It is an image, not of fragility, but of poise: poised between the divine infinite incomprehensibility above us, where leads the bridge, which is the creative Word, and the abyss of our own nothingness, from which we have come, and to which we could condemn ourselves.

The notion of a fundamental divide between God and creatures is open to misunderstanding – an easy misunderstanding owing to the obtuseness of our imagination. It could easily suggest an infinite chasm between God and the creature, making God seem utterly remote from his creation. But that would be to take the image of a divide, or a gulf, in too physical a way. A physical gulf does separate, hold apart. But, as we have seen, God and creatures do not belong to some overarching category of reality within which they are separated from one another; God is beyond any creaturely categories, and so can be thought of as infinitely exalted, when we consider that his being is utterly unlike ours, but also infinitely close, for the same reason. He is, as St Augustine put it, *interior intimo meo et superior summo meo*, 'more inward than my inmost self and higher than my highest self'.[15] Creation out of nothing does indeed mean that the created order does not flow from within God's

---

[13] *De Incarnatione* 4.

[14] Philaret (Drozdov) of Moscow, Sermon on the Discovery of the Relics of St Aleksii, Metropolitan of Moscow and Wonderworker, given 29 May 1830, *Izbrannye Trudy Pisma Vospominaniya* (Moscow: St Tikhon's Orthodox Theological Institute, 2003), 268. This passage is quoted by both Lossky and Florovsky.

[15] Augustine, *Confessions* III. 6. 11.

being, as it were, as some kind of extension or emanation of his being, but it does not mean that creation is remote from the divine.[16] On the contrary, God is intimately present to all his creatures.

This is a fundamental intuition within the Orthodox tradition, which is sometimes fearful (maybe with good reason) that the Western Christian tradition has not preserved such a profound sense of God's presence to his creation. Both the idea of nature as independent of grace and supernature, as if creation itself is not a gracious gift of God, and the notion, widely accepted nowadays, that we live in a disenchanted world: both of these seem to the Orthodox tradition to be fundamentally wrong. Orthodox theology has developed several ways of expressing the conviction of God's presence to his creation; we might consider three of them: the notion of God's activities or energies, the idea of the *logoi* or principles of creation, and the doctrine of the Wisdom of God, sophiology, that was popular in the Russian tradition at the turn of the nineteenth/twentieth century.

Essence and energies

The distinction between God's essence and energies (this is the term used by most Orthodox theologians writing in English, though 'activity' seems to me a much better translation of the Greek *energeia*) became an established distinction in the theology of St Gregory Palamas. He justified this distinction by appeal to earlier Greek theologians, such as Basil the Great and Maximos the Confessor, though the systematic use of the distinction seems to be Gregory's (and indeed he only gradually came to realize its value). The distinction between essence and energies is a distinction between God in himself and God in his activity; God in himself, in his essence, *ousia*, is

---

[16] The question of the meaning of creation *ex nihilo* has been a matter of debate in recent Orthodox theology. See the exchange between Metropolitan John (Zizioulas) of Pergamon and Philip Sherrard, printed in John D. Zizioulas, *Communion and Otherness* (London: T. & T. Clark, 2006), 270–85. The article by Zizioulas that provoked the correspondence is reprinted in *Communion*, 250–69. For an exposition of Sherrard's own position, see his 'The Meaning of Creation *ex nihilo*', in *Christianity: Lineaments of a Sacred Tradition* (Brookline, MA: Holy Cross Orthodox Press, 1997), 232–44, to be read in conjunction with the immediately preceding chapter, 'Christianity and the Desecration of the Cosmos', 200–231. Some of Sherrard's concerns are met, I hope, in what follows.

unknowable, but in his activities or energies he makes himself known. Gregory insists that these energies are not created effects of God's activity, but are the uncreated God himself active within his creation: when we encounter God in his energies, we are not encountering God at one remove, as it were, we are encountering God himself.

The context in which Gregory developed this distinction was his defence of the monks of the Holy Mountain, called 'hesychasts' (from the Greek *hesychia*, meaning 'quietness', 'tranquillity') because of their commitment to silent prayer, who claimed in their prayer to experience God himself in the form of transfiguring light. Gregory maintained, against their opponents, that this light was not a created phenomenon, still less an hallucination, but the uncreated light of the Godhead, one of God's energies, the light that radiated from Christ at the Transfiguration, and in encountering the uncreated light, the hesychasts were encountering God himself, indeed finding union with God. But the distinction can be employed more widely: everywhere in Creation, because everything comes immediately from the hand of the Creator, it is possible to encounter God in his energies. Some Orthodox theologians have been happy to use the word 'panentheism' ('all-in-God'-ness), in contradistinction from pantheism (in which everything is identified with God), and Orthodox theologians are among the earliest in their use of this term.

Logoi of creation

The notion of the *logoi* of creation is mostly associated with the great Byzantine theologian, St Maximos the Confessor, though one can trace the idea back to Origen (and indeed Plotinos and behind him the Stoics), and it was developed by Evagrios, on whom Maximos drew. According to St John's Gospel, all things were made through the *Logos*, or Word of God (John 1.3). The term *logos* is in Greek a key term, difficult to translate into other languages, because it has such a wide range of connotations: it can mean word, reason, meaning, principle, definition. So the *Logos* of God, through whom the universe has been created, is both the word, utterance, of God the Father, and also the meaning of the universe, and the meaning of everything in the universe. To say that the cosmos was created by the *Logos* of the Father is not just to say that it was created by God, but also to suggest that the meaning of the cosmos is to be found in the *Logos*.

41

The Stoics had already thought in terms of the *logos* as the meaning of the cosmos, and also of many seeds of the *logos* as expressing the multiple levels of meaning found throughout the cosmos. In Maximos, we find the idea that everything in the universe has its meaning in its own *logos*, or principle, but that all these *logoi* form a coherent whole, because they all participate in the one *Logos* of God, the *Logos* or Word of God that became incarnate in our Lord Jesus Christ. Maximos is fond of repeating that 'the one *Logos* is the many *logoi*, and the many *logoi* are the one *Logos*'.[17] This means that the meaning of the universe can be found in Christ; from which he develops a notion of the cosmic Christ, revealed and celebrated in the cosmic liturgy.[18] But Maximos is equally interested in the other side of the doctrine of the *logoi* of Creation: his conviction that everything finds its meaning in its *logos* of being, *logos tes ousias*, which in turn participates in the *Logos* of God. Consequently, for Maximos, each being finds its meaning in its nature, in what it is intended to be, as defined by the *logos* of being, and this *logos* of being is inviolable: the meanings of all the created beings coinhere, for 'the many *logoi* are the one *Logos*'.

This notion of a coinherence of interlocking *logoi* has attracted the attention of some scientists in the last century and this: here is a vision of the cosmos that takes seriously the integrity of natural entities, and sees their meanings as converging in a single coherent vision. Furthermore, the human has a pivotal role in the perception of this ultimate meaning, for Maximos sees the human as reflecting the cosmos in himself and the cosmos as reflected in the human, regarding the human as a microcosm, a little cosmos, and indeed the cosmos as a macranthropos, a large human. The human is seen as a bond of the cosmos, *syndesmos tou kosmou*. These ideas were common currency in much of the philosophy of his time, but Maximos gives it his own twist by rooting the role of the human as bond of the cosmos in the doctrine of the human as created in the image of God.

---

[17] Especially in *Ambiguum* 7, which is translated in St Maximus the Confessor, *On the Cosmic Mystery of Jesus Christ* (trans. Paul Blowers and Robert Louis Wilson; Crestwood, NY: St Vladimir's Seminary Press, 2003), which has an excellent introduction by Paul Blowers.

[18] The title of an historic book on Maximos the Confessor by Hans Urs von Balthasar, *Cosmic Liturgy: The Universe according to Maximus the Confessor* (San Francisco: Ignatius Press, 2003; German original 1941; much expanded and rewritten second edn 1961; Eng. trans. Brian E. Daley SJ from the 3rd German edn 1988).

The idea of the human as the image of God is central to any patristic understanding of what it is to be human, and we shall return to it several times in future chapters, but here its importance is that the human, as the image of God, fulfils within the cosmos the divine role of providing meaning for the cosmos. This can be explored in various ways – and is central, as we shall see, to an Orthodox understanding of sin and the Fall – but the idea that the human is central to any grasp of the cosmic has become important in many attempts by scientists to formulate some universal theory of the meaning of the universe. Maximos' doctrine of the *logoi* has seemed to some a powerful way of articulating some sense of how the universe can be seen as meaningful. Not only that, such a vision of the cosmos provides a basis for developing a response to the ecological problems that press upon us, for here we have a view of the cosmos that finds intrinsic meaning in the cosmos, and prevents any understanding of it as inert material to be exploited by human ingenuity. Furthermore, the notion of the human as bond of the cosmos highlights human responsibility for the cosmos.[19]

Sophiology

Sophiology, the doctrine associated with the Russian religious philosophers at the end of the nineteenth and the beginning of the twentieth centuries – especially Vladimir Solov'ev, Pavel Florensky and Sergii Bulgakov – can also be seen as an attempt to articulate a sense of God's presence to, and yet distinction from, the cosmos. For most of those who advocated sophiology, it was bound up with their own experiences – of nature, of human love. Bulgakov tells of an experience he had while still an atheist Marxist:

> One evening we were driving across the southern steppes of Russia, and the strong-scented spring grass was gilded by the rays of a glorious sunset. Far in the distance I saw the blue outlines of the Caucasus. This was my first sight of the mountains. I looked with ecstatic delight at their rising slopes. I drank in the light and the air of the steppes.

---

[19] A concern for ecology, rooted in the tradition of the Orthodox Church, has been one of the distinctive features of Patriarch Bartholomew's mission as Patriarch: see *On Earth as in Heaven: Ecological Vision and Initiatives of Ecumenical Patriarch Bartholomew* (ed. John Chryssavgis; New York: Fordham University Press, 2012).

I listened to the revelation of nature. My soul was accustomed to the dull pain of seeing nature as a lifeless desert and of treating its surface beauty as a deceptive mask. Yet, contrary to my intellectual convictions, I could not be reconciled to nature without God.[20]

For Bulgakov, to accept the delight of the natural world and to believe in God were to go together; only if God exists, can nature be seen as enchanted. It was that conviction that made sophiology so important for him.

Sophiology has experienced something of a revival in the last decade, especially among the movement in modern theology known as 'radical orthodoxy'.[21] It is, nevertheless, still the case that in (authentically) Orthodox circles, sophiology is treated with suspicion, and even those willing to be sympathetic towards Bulgakov often take the line that everything he wants to say using the notion of divine Sophia could be said just as adequately without invoking the notion of Wisdom or Sophia. (Bulgakov's late work, *The Orthodox Church*, in which he gives an account of Orthodox beliefs without using the notion of Sophia, is cited in support of such an opinion.) It may well be true that Sophia can be dispensed with, if one understands doctrine as a string of theological positions. It is rather as one tries to understand their coherence and mutual entailments that Sophia comes into its own for Bulgakov.

The fundamental intuition of sophiology is relatively easy to enunciate. It is that the gulf between the uncreated God and creation, brought into being out of nothing, does not put creation in opposition to God; rather, Wisdom constitutes a kind of *metaxu*,[22] 'between': between God and man/creation, for Wisdom is that through which God created the universe, and it is equally through wisdom that the human quest for God finds fulfilment.[23] Wisdom, one might say, is the

---

[20] From his *Autobiographical Sketches*; trans. in *A Bulgakov Anthology: Sergius Bulgakov 1871–1944* (ed. James Pain and Nicolas Zernov; London: SPCK, 1976), 10.

[21] My awareness of this has been greatly enhanced by the work of Brandon Gallaher, and conversation with him. See his 'Graced Creatureliness: Ontological Tension in the Uncreated/Created Distinction in the Sophiologies of Solov'ev, Bulgakov and Milbank', *Logos: A Journal of Eastern Christian Studies* 47 (2006), 163–90.

[22] Palamas uses the same (Platonic?) term for the uncreated manifold participating in God, but not the divine essence itself: *Triads* III. 2. 25.

[23] For a longer account of my approach to Bulgakov's doctrine of Sophia, see 'Wisdom and the Russians: The Sophiology of Fr Sergei Bulgakov', in *Where Shall Wisdom Be Found?* (ed. Stephen C. Barton; Edinburgh: T. & T. Clark, 1999), 169–81.

face that God turns towards his creation, and the face that creation, in human kind, turns towards God. Creation is not abandoned by God, it is not godless, for apart from God it would not be at all; it is not deprived of grace, for it owes its existence to grace. Rather, creation is graced, it is holy; in creation God may be encountered.

Bulgakov's account of his experience in the Caucasus, just quoted – and his magnificent account of standing beneath the dome of the Church of Hagia Sophia in Constantinople in January 1923[24] – make clear how important this intuition was to him. It also lay at the heart of what he perceived to be wrong with the Roman Catholicism he encountered in the West as an exile: the idea of an ungraced 'pure nature', a key term in the Thomism of the day, seemed to him fundamentally false. The relationship between God and the world, constituted by Wisdom, cannot be an arbitrary relationship, nor can it be a necessary one. Uncreated wisdom and created wisdom differ only in being uncreated or created. Why? Because if they differed in any other way, God would be severed from creation and creation from God. This line of thought indicates a further step involved in sophiology, which raises the issue: What must creation be, if this is true? What is creation like, if God indeed created it (through wisdom)?

Thus we find ourselves asking questions that have exercised Christians for centuries, and perhaps most acutely when, in the second century, Christianity faced the manifold challenges of Greek philosophy and gnosticism. Christianity was not consonant with just any view of the universe. Christians agreed with the Platonists over the existence of a transcendent divine, the co-existence of divine providence and human free will, and adopted Platonist arguments against other Greek philosophers – Aristotelians, Stoics and Epicureans – who rejected one or other of these positions.[25] They felt a profound affinity with the Stoic notion of the cosmos as an harmonious unity. They completely rejected the view, held by most of those whom scholars now call 'Gnostics', that the universe was the product of a God or gods who were either malevolent or negligent. Sophiology was, for Bulgakov, a way of articulating what it means for the cosmos

---

[24] While still a mosque. See *A Bulgakov Anthology*, 13–14.

[25] See my 'Pagans and Christians on Providence', in *Texts and Culture in Late Antiquity: Inheritance, Authority and Change* (ed. J. H. D. Scourfield; Swansea: Classical Press of Wales, 2007), 279–97.

to be God's creation, both in the sense of what kind of world that must be – a moral universe in which human freedom is the key to the discovery of meaning – and in the sense that the pursuit of wisdom through exploring the cosmos – the physical cosmos, certainly, but also the moral and spiritual world opened up by human interaction with the cosmos – could lead to an encounter with the divine.

Angels and demons

The created order consists of 'heaven and earth, things visible and invisible': the human stands at, or constitutes, the boundary, *methorion*, between the visible and the invisible, the earthly and the heavenly, the material and the spiritual. The human is spiritual, but is embodied; is earthly, but aspires to heaven; he is a rational animal – part of the animal world – and yet participating in the *Logos* and therefore *logikos*, rational (though *logikos* is a much more suggestive word than 'rational'). But there are other rational, *logikoi*, beings: angels and, alas, demons. These, too, are part of the created order.

It is perhaps in the divine liturgy that the sense of the presence of the angels is most keenly felt. As the holy gifts are carried through the church from the table of preparation to the holy table, we sing the Cherubic hymn:

> We who in a mystery represent the Cherubim and sing the thrice-holy hymn to the life-giving Trinity, let us now lay aside every care of this life. For we are about to receive the King of all, invisibly escorted by the angelic hosts. Alleluia, alleluia, alleluia![26]

And when we come to sing the thrice-holy hymn in the eucharistic prayer, we recall the 'thousands of Archangels and ten thousands of angels, the Cherubim and the Seraphim, six-winged and many-eyed, soaring upon their wings, singing, crying, shouting the triumphal hymn'.[27] All this evokes the vision of the prophet Isaias, who saw

> the Lord sitting upon a throne, high and lifted up; and the house was full of his glory. The seraphim stood around him; the one had six wings and the other had six wings, and with two they covered their face, with two they covered their feet and with two they flew. And they cried out

---

[26] *Liturgy of St John Chrysostom*, 22.
[27] *Liturgy of St John Chrysostom*, 31.

to each other and said: Holy, holy, holy is the Lord of Sabaoth; the whole earth is full of his glory. (Isa. 6.1–3)

As we come into the presence of God, pre-eminently in worship, we are made aware of the presence of the angelic hosts that stand before God. It is as if the angels are the sparks that fly off as God and his Creation encounter each other.

It is in the Temple, the place of meeting between God and humans, on those occasions when humans encounter God, such as Abraham's encounter with God at the Oak of Mamre (Gen. 18) or Jacob's dream (Gen. 28.12–17), that we find mention of angels in the Old Testament. We have already seen the mention of angels in the Temple, in Isaias' vision; Abraham encounters God in the form of three angels, and the chapter ends with the moving story of Abraham pleading with God for the people of Sodom; Jacob in his dream sees a ladder set up from earth to heaven, with the angels of God ascending and descending upon it – he wakes up, and exclaims: 'Surely the Lord is in this place; and I did not know it . . . How awesome is this place! This is none other than the house of God, and this is the gate of heaven.'

So in the New Testament: the Lord himself sums up the significance of the Incarnation to Nathanael by saying that he will see 'heaven opened and the angels of God ascending and descending upon the Son of man' (John 1.51). At the annunciation of the Incarnation to the blessed Virgin, there is an archangel, Gabriel; at the nativity of the Lord, the angel announces the event to the shepherds, 'and suddenly there was with the angel a multitude of heavenly hosts praising God' (Luke 2.13); as the Lord prays in the Garden of Gethsemane, 'an angel from heaven strengthened him' (Luke 22.43); in the Empty Tomb, it is an angel who announces to the women, 'he is not here, but is risen' (Matt. 28.6). And angels continue to appear throughout the life of the Church; several miracles associated with angels are commemorated in the liturgical year.

As one reflects on all this, one has the sense of another world, an unseen presence, a sense that we are not alone. Two passages in the Scriptures seem to me to convey this with a peculiar force. In the fourth book of Kingdoms (2 Kings in Western Bibles), Eliseus and his servant wake up one morning to find the Syrian army surrounding them. His servant is alarmed, but Eliseus tells him, 'Fear not, for those who are with us are more than those who are with them'; and the servant's eyes are opened to see 'the mountain . . . full of horses and chariots of fire round about Eliseus' (4 Kgdms 6.16–17). And then in the first epistle of John: 'Little children, you are of God, and have overcome them; for he who is in you is greater than he who is in the world' (1 John 4.4). We are like Eliseus' servant; and the one who is with us is Christ himself.

Orthodox services and prayer books also have prayers to our guardian angel.[28] It is an ancient belief that each of us, at our baptism, is assigned a guardian angel, whose duty is to look after us, to warn us if we seem to be straying from the path of discipleship to Christ. This is a further expression of the belief that, though much is demanded of us individually, we are not on our own: the saints pray for us, especially our patron saint whose name we were given in baptism, and the angels watch over us, especially our guardian angel.

As the Church reflected on the ministry of the angels, it came to assimilate them to the beings intermediate between gods and men. The Greeks called them *daimones*, which we transliterate as demons, a little unfortunately, as there was nothing essentially evil about *daimones*; like human beings, some were well-disposed, some ill-disposed. Somewhere it is commented that angels is the word the Scriptures use to designate those the Greeks called *daimones*. This notion of beings intermediary between God and humans comes to take the form of thinking of angels as created, rational beings, like humans, but bodiless (or at least with much more ethereal bodies); the visible forms ascribed to them are either symbolic or adopted in order to communicate with humans (or indeed both). Speculation about what was meant by the different terms used in Scripture of these celestial beings – angels, archangels, principalities and powers, authorities, thrones, seraphim and cherubim – was eventually settled by the near-universal acceptance of the picture of the celestial beings found in the writings of one who wrote under the name of Dionysios the Areopagite, the judge of the Areopagos in Athens converted by the apostle Paul (cf. Acts 17). According to him, the celestial beings are ranked three by three – at the top: seraphim, cherubim, thrones (in descending order); in the middle: dominions, powers, authorities; at the bottom: principalities, archangels, angels.

---

[28] For example: *An Orthodox Prayer Book* (Eng. trans. Archimandrite Ephrem Lash; Milton under Wychwood: Fellowship of St Alban & St Sergius, 2009), 31.

The terminology – angels and demons – at first simply terms of different background (biblical or classical) for intermediary beings, came to develop in Christian usage into an opposition: angels were good beings, and demons bad. This was perhaps inspired by the use in the Gospels of the diminutive, *daimonion*, for the demons opposed to Christ, and perhaps also by the pagan theory that the gods manifest in sacred statues, or idols, as Christians saw them, were *daimones*, representing the gods. By the fourth century, at least, angels and demons in Christian usage are opposed beings. Within the monastic and ascetic tradition, especially, demons are associated with the temptations that face Christians seeking to follow the gospel, so that the struggle against temptation and sin is presented as warfare between humans and demons. It is too large a topic to treat here, but Christian experience has been that the struggle against sin and temptation is not so much like a struggle with one's own propensities, but more like warfare, in which we are pitted against a foe that seeks to outwit us.

Belief in angels and demons is not something that fits very well with the 'modern mind', but its place in traditional Orthodox thinking is not superficial.[29] At the very least, openness to the reality of such beings might remind us that, in Hamlet's words, 'There are more things in heaven and earth, . . . Than are dreamt of in your philosophy'.

---

[29] See, recently, Andrei Pleşu, *Actualité des anges* (Paris: Buchet Chastel, 2003), soon to be available in English.

4

Who is Christ?

Christ and the Gospels

We come to the central chapter of this book, in which we look at what we believe, as Orthodox Christians, about Christ. The whole question of what we know about Christ, and how we know it, has been made complicated – at least at an intellectual level – by three centuries of argument and scholarship in the West. The sources seem obvious – principally, the four Gospels that we find in the New Testament – but modern Western scholarship, mostly Protestant, has made what seems obvious shadowy and ambiguous.

Very simply, the argument has gone something like this. The four Gospels are not direct eye-witness accounts of the life of Christ. The literary relationships between the Gospels, and the kind of material we find in the Gospels, make it clear, it is argued, that we are dealing with an oral tradition that was not written down until several decades after Christ's death. Even at the stage of writing down, it looks as if this material was used very freely. Mark's Gospel, it is claimed, is the earliest, and was used in different ways by the authors of Matthew and Luke. They also supplemented the material from Mark with other material, some of which both authors used, and some of which seems to have been special to each of the two Evangelists.

The case of the fourth Gospel, attributed to St John, is different again: a difference that has long been recognized – Clement of Alexandria called it the 'spiritual Gospel'. There is a lot of argument as to how much John knew of the other, so-called Synoptic Gospels, but the idea that he was independent of them looks less and less likely, in which case the differences – in chronology and the interpretation of events – need some explanation. Very quickly we seem to find ourselves confronted with a kind of complex palimpsest of traditions, raising difficult questions of authenticity.

A further problem for Protestant scholarship is that the four Gospels have been revered as such because, in some way, the details of which are obscure to us, towards the end of the second century – a century and a half after the death of Christ – the Church set its seal on these Gospels, and rejected other texts as being inauthentic.[1] The ground of the Church's decision seems to have been 'apostolicity', meaning, at least, that the four Gospels could be traced back to apostles: Matthew and John were among the Twelve Apostles, and it was maintained that Mark had the authority of the apostle Peter, and Luke the authority of the apostle Paul (not, historically, one of the Twelve, but quickly regarded as an apostle on a par with the Twelve). Modern scholars have had difficulty in maintaining the authenticity of these attributions and within Protestantism appeal to the authority of the Church seems to turn on its head the Reformation principle of the authority of Scripture over against the Church. So the authority of the four Gospels becomes unclear.

Where do we Orthodox stand in relation to this? Is there, indeed, an 'Orthodox' position? Isn't it simply a matter of scholarship?

Christ and the resurrection

I think there is an Orthodox position on the Gospels, and it is one we share with other Christians, not least the Roman Catholics, though it may be we find it easier to articulate than others. I would argue that there are two points we need to take into account, that are overlooked by the way the debate over the Gospels has been conducted by scholars. First of all – and suggested by the title of this chapter – the question is not: Who *was* Christ? but: Who *is* Christ?

We are not asking about the life story and teaching of a dead man, we are asking about someone whom we believe to be alive today. We believe in the resurrection. You might say – and some scholars certainly would – that this is putting the cart before the horse. The

---

[1] I should perhaps spell out that we really know nothing for certain about the formation of what has come to be known as the Canon of Scripture, or at least about the process that led to this. To begin with 'Scripture' meant the Scriptures of the Hebrews, which Christians seem to have read in the Septuagint version. To this is added, by the end of the second century, the four Gospels and the writings of the 'Apostles', first of all, the epistles of Paul, then other apostles – James, Peter, John and Jude; the lists of received writings seem to have varied, for some centuries. It was, however, certainly a matter of a decision taken by those who saw themselves as representing the 'Church', though it is most unlikely that this involved any formal procedure – a formally constituted synod, for example. We certainly have no knowledge of such.

event of the resurrection needs evidence, and yet I am saying that
it is only in the light of the resurrection that we can approach the
evidence of the Gospels. But, in fact, this is a truism. Everyone accepts
that the Gospels were written in the light of the resurrection; nobody
thinks that they present us with unvarnished facts on the basis of
which we can make up our minds. It simply is not the case, and no
one really thinks that it is, that we can decide the truth of Christianity
by sitting down and sorting out the historical evidence, and then
making our own decision. It just isn't like that.

The Gospels themselves, in fact, contain hints about this. Twice
in St John's Gospel we are told that its writer, the 'beloved disciple'
(identified with John by a process of elimination), is the witness of
these things, and 'we know that his witness is true'. Witness to what?
Essentially to the death and resurrection of Christ (see John 19.35;
21.14; cf. 20.31). The beloved disciple is presented as one who was
close to Christ and can tell us about the One we believe in: his
teaching and the truth of his death and resurrection. The idea that
something is involved beyond our own assessment of the historical
facts is there in the final scene in Matthew's Gospel: when the Lord
appears after the resurrection to the 11 disciples, on a mountain, it
is said that 'when they saw him they worshipped him; but some of
them doubted' (Matt. 28.17). John tells a similar story with his account
of Thomas' doubts about the resurrection: it is the personal encounter
with the Lord that convinces Thomas (John 20.24–29). Faith in the
resurrection is not about assessing some historical fact, it is about
encountering the Risen Lord, One who, as risen, is alive.

Christ and the apostolic witness

The other point we need to take into account is this. Modern scholarship has made clear that we cannot go behind the Gospels as authenti-
cated by the Church to some historical documents, or other evidence,
that give us the unvarnished facts. If we try to discount the faith in
Christ's resurrection of the Christians who preserved these stories,
and eventually put them together in the Gospels, then we shall find
that we are discounting virtually everything: there will be nothing
left for us on which to make our own judgements.

That is a disaster to a certain kind of Protestant, and can lead to
an understanding of faith as so utterly paradoxical that it would

actually be compromised, if there were more historical evidence to support it: we find this kind of position in Kierkegaard, and later in the New Testament scholar, Rudolf Bultmann. But from another point of view it is scarcely a problem at all. What we are being told, in effect, is that the Gospels preserve the witness of the early Christians, and especially the apostles, to faith in Christ, and his death and resurrection. It is only if we *mistrust* the apostles that this becomes a problem. If we cannot accept the witness of the apostles, we have nowhere to go: but is that surprising? To be a Christian is not to be an individual who has made up his or her own mind about the reliability of the Gospels; to be a Christian is to be part of the Church, Christ's body, and to find as we trust one another within that community, that we come to encounter Christ.

That encounter with Christ can take many forms. Metropolitan Anthony of Sourozh encountered Christ through the experience of reading St Mark's Gospel and feeling that Christ was there with him, as he read.[2] For others it is not so easy to put one's finger on any event like that, but nonetheless it is in the community of the Church that we find we know the love of Christ, and of his friends, the saints: we know this as a real experience of living persons. Moreover, if we can trust the community of faith in which we find ourselves, we can trace the lineaments of that trust through the life of the Church to the band of disciples that accompanied Christ in his lifetime, and were witnesses of his resurrection.

It seems to me that modern biblical scholarship has only shown us the stark truth that Christianity finds its beginning in faith in the resurrection: faith, not in the sense of a paradoxical commitment that reposes on nothing, but faith in the sense of trust in the community of faith that is the Church. If that is true, then it seems to me that it does not matter too much whether Matthew, for instance, was an apostle: the Gospel was attributed to him because the Church felt it was fundamentally apostolic, and in some way Matthaean, maybe because some of the stories concerned him. It is, if you like, rather the case that it was because the witness of that Gospel was felt to be genuinely apostolic that the Church was happy about its attribution to Matthew, not because Matthew actually wrote it. With

---

[2] Cf. Gillian Crow, *'This Holy Man': Impressions of Metropolitan Anthony* (London: Darton, Longman & Todd, 2005), 40–1.

those Gospels – the so-called apocryphal Gospels – that did not receive the Church's seal of approval, their claims to be by apostles such as Thomas or Peter were rejected, because their doctrine was not recognized as apostolic.

Death and Christ's voluntary passion

How, then, are we to read the witness of the Gospels – and of the New Testament, more broadly – to Jesus of Nazareth, the Christ? It is abundantly clear that it is from the perspective of the death and resurrection of Christ that we are to read these works. The death of Christ is so important because it is death that has cast its pall over human life, and indeed over the life of the cosmos. Death is the problem that needs to be answered: death that calls in question everything we try to achieve, death that seems to be the inevitable horizon of human life. No remedy for the human condition that falls short of death is of any use.

The verses that we sing during Holy Week in the Orthodox liturgy speak a great deal about Christ's 'voluntary passion'. Every service between Palm Sunday evening and Holy Thursday ends with the priest's blessing which begins: 'May the Lord who is coming to his voluntary passion [*to hekousion pathos*] . . .' There is a kind of deliberate contradiction – or paradox – in that expression. For a *pathos* is essentially something that happens to us, that overwhelms us, that we suffer, whereas what is voluntary is something that we do. We do not decide to die: it is the ultimate *pathos*, something that happens to us.

But not, we believe, in the case of Christ. Even in the Synoptic Gospels, Jesus is presented not as someone to whom things happen, but as one who stamps his own character on events; in the fourth Gospel it is explicit – 'no one takes [my life] from me, but I lay it down of my own accord' (John 10.18) – or as we hear in the Liturgy of St John Chrysostom: 'in the night in which he was given up, *or rather gave himself up*, for the life of the world'.[3] And so in the case of his death: Christ does not succumb to death, but rather encounters death and overthrows it; he descends into the place of the dead, Hades or hell, and liberates those who had been held there since Adam,

---

[3] *The Divine Liturgy of our Father among the Saints John Chrysostom* (Oxford: Oxford University Press, 1995), 32 (my italics).

beginning with Adam and Eve, as we see in the icon of the resurrection, or the *Anastasis*. 'Love is as strong as death', we read in the Song of Songs (Cant. 8.6), and here that observation takes on a new meaning: Christ's love for human kind is able to overcome death, for it does not succumb to death, but seeks it out.

This belief that Christ did not succumb to death, but overcame death: something manifest in the resurrection, when he demonstrates that death has not taken him, but he has overthrown death – it is this that is the fundamental Christian belief. Because it is death that Christ has overthrown – death that reduces all our efforts to nothing – Christ is shown to be beyond the reach of any power that could threaten us. So the apostle Paul affirms:

> I am sure that neither death, nor life, nor angels, nor principalities, nor things present, nor things to come, nor powers, nor height, nor depth, nor anything else in all creation, will be able to separate us from the love of God in Christ Jesus our Lord. (Rom. 8.38–39)

A love more powerful than 'anything else in all creation': already Paul had probably drawn from that the conclusion that the one who had died on the cross, the Lord Jesus Christ, is one 'through whom are all things and through whom we exist' (1 Cor. 8.6). It is an amazing statement: that one who had died barely 20 years earlier was the one through whom all things came into being. For the apostle Paul it had to be true, because otherwise it would be impossible to explain how there is nothing in all creation that can threaten the 'love of God in Christ Jesus our Lord'. The one who had died on the cross was evidently a man; but the nature of that death, and the consequences of that death, demonstrated that he transcended creation: and this is the case, because it was through him that everything had been created.

Christ and prayer

But there are other, more personal, ways in which the Lord of the Gospels was seen to be more than simply human. It is beyond the scope of the present study to pursue this in more detail, but I want to explore briefly one of these ways. Throughout the Gospels, Jesus is shown as a man of prayer. He rises early and prays (Mark 1.35); on one striking occasion, we are told that the Lord went up into a mountain to pray while his disciples crossed the Lake of Galilee and got caught in a storm during the night; just before dawn the Lord appeared to his disciples on the water and dismissed the storm (Matt. 14.23–33; Mark 46—52; John 6.15–21). Luke, in particular, mentions the Lord as praying at the time of his baptism (Luke 3.21) and at the Transfiguration (Luke 9.28). Jesus teaches his disciples to pray, and gives them the Lord's Prayer, the 'Our Father' (Matt. 6.7–13; Luke 11.1–4). Finally, before his passion, the Lord prays in the Garden of Gethsemane (Matt. 26.36–46; Mark 14.32–42; Luke 22.40–46).

In drawing attention to the prayer of Christ, the Evangelists are drawing attention to his humanity, for prayer is how human beings relate to God. The human-ness of Christ is perhaps especially manifest in the prayer of the agony in Gethsemane: 'Abba, Father, all things are possible to you. Let this cup pass from me. Nevertheless not what I will, but what you will' (Mark 14.36). (It is interesting to note, in passing, how much Luke makes us see the parallel between the prayer of the agony, and the Lord's Prayer: addressing God as simply 'Father', as in the Lucan version of the 'Our Father', twice exhorting the disciples to prayer against entering temptation [the closing petition of Luke's 'Our Father'], and the echo of 'Your will be done . . .' [a strongly attested reading in Luke's version] in the Lord's Prayer in the Garden.) But even in the Gospel accounts, Jesus is manifest as more than human: not in the sense of super-human, but as, in some way, one to whom we relate *as God*. The most obvious places are the occasion in Matthew's Gospel, where Jesus turns from prayer to his Father, and turns to – well, it is not exactly clear whom, and that may be the point – saying,

> Come to me all who labour and are burdened, and I will give you rest. Take your yoke on me and learn of me, because I am gentle and humble of heart, and you will find rest for your souls; for my yoke is easy and my burden is light.   (Matt. 11.28)

and the account of the Transfiguration, where the Lord appears transfigured in glory (Matt. 17.1–8; Mark 9.2–8; Luke 9.28–36). This account – like that of the Baptism of Christ, 'where the worship of the Trinity was made manifest' (apolytikion for the Theophany) – reveals the Lord declared to be the 'Son' of the Father.

The idea that Jesus unites in himself sonship in two ways – as 'Son of Man', understood by the Fathers to mean 'one among human sons', and 'Son of God', begotten by the Father – we have already encountered. It is adumbrated in both these passages, and developed in the fourth Gospel: there the Lord is the Son of the Father, sent into the world; here in the world, we can enfold our prayer in his, but at the same time, he is one who manifests the Father ('He who has seen me has seen the Father', John 14.9), and to whom the disciples (and first of all his own mother, John 2.5) turn in prayer, finally and openly in the apostle Thomas' exclamation, 'My Lord and my God' (John 20.28). Jesus is then presented as the one to whom we pray – as God the Son, within the life of the Trinity; as well as one in whose prayers ours can be enfolded – as man.

The dogma of Christ

Out of this perception, there emerged the doctrine of Christ as one person in two perfect natures, divine and human. It is the realization of this doctrine, and the working out of its implications, that came to be the central preoccupation of the Œcumenical Councils of the Church: councils that are of enduring importance in the life of the Church. I want now briefly to trace this history, from the first to the eighth century.[4] It is not exactly the *development* of a doctrine, to use the term popularized by Newman: that gives the impression of some kind of evolution, with the Church's faith changing and even getting better, as if we in the twenty-first century know the faith more deeply than St Paul, say. I prefer to talk in terms of realization, rather than development: a growing clarity, not deeper insights. The only growing in depth that matters is a growing in depth in our relationship with God in Christ through the Holy Spirit. I do not doubt the truth of Newman's words, 'In a higher world it is otherwise; but here below to live is to change, and to be perfect is to have changed often';[5] but they apply, it seems to me, to our own development as persons, not to the Church as the body of Christ. If there is a history of doctrine, it is (as one of my Greek pupils once pointed out to me) the history of heresy, which is constantly changing, not a history of the faith of the Church.

---

[4] For a somewhat more extended, though still brief, account see my *St John Damascene: Tradition and Originality in Byzantine Theology* (Oxford: Oxford University Press, 2002), 147–55.

[5] J. H. Newman, *An Essay on the Development of Christian Doctrine* (The Edition of 1845; ed. J. M. Cameron; Harmondsworth: Penguin, 1974), 100.

Put simply, the Church confesses about Christ that he is the Son of God become human, become a man, without ceasing to be God. The history of Christology is the history of the attempt to preserve that confession. Perhaps the first problem was to square the attribution of some kind of divinity to Christ with the monotheism of the Hebrew religion in the bosom of which Christianity was formed. In the first century or so, Christians came to realize that what distinguished them from other Jews was their belief that the promised Messiah, the Christ, had come; that the messianic age had dawned. But this messiah manifested his power on the cross; he was no political champion of Israel's hopes. Rather, what he achieved was something much deeper: it was, as we have seen, the overthrow of death and all the ways in which death has corrupted human life, and the life of the world as a whole. Already one can see a revision of what divine power looks like – not coercion, but love – which further entails that the anointed one of the Jews, the Messiah, was the fulfilment of the hopes of all humanity: 'a light for revelation to the nations, and the glory of your people Israel', in the words of Symeon, who carried the child Jesus in his arms when he was presented in the Temple (Luke 2.32). Ideas about the real meaning of divinity – of who or what God is – subverted the normal expectations of both Jews and Gentiles: love and faithfulness revealed the nature of God, not power and dominion.

Nonetheless, the Hebrew belief that there was one God, not the pantheon of Mediterranean paganism, was a conviction that the Christian tradition endorsed. In some way, acknowledgment of Christ had to be an expression of monotheism, not its contradiction. In the end, Christians came to speak of a Triad, or Trinity, that did not compromise the divine unity. Apart from those who either abandoned the unity of God or understood it very elastically – some groups among those scholars often call 'Gnostics' – we find either a stress on the unity of God that saw Christ as no more than an exceptionally blessed human being, or an understanding of the Godhead as including a hidden, unknowable dimension, called the 'Father', as well as another dimension, through which God communicated with the world, without losing his hiddenness.

It is this last notion that eventually became dominant in the third century: what scholars call *logos* theology, the idea that God, as he communicates himself, does so as *logos*. This Greek word covers reason, meaning, communication – something that in popularized

Stoic thought made the cosmos precisely *kosmos*, that is, ordered, harmonious, beautiful (*kosmos* is the root from which the modern word 'cosmetic' is derived). What Christians claimed about Christ could be put in this way: that in Christ we encounter the meaning of the universe, or better, the one who gives meaning to the cosmos.

The *logos* theology also recognized that glimpses of the truth, seeds of the *logos*, could be found in the philosophers of the classical past, especially Socrates and Plato, so that their insights could be incorporated into the Christian understanding of things. Such reflection on the *logos* found a lot of encouragement in the beginning of the fourth Gospel, with its proclamation that

> In the beginning was the Word or Logos, and the Word was with God, and the Word was God. Everything came into being through him . . . And the Word became flesh and dwelt among us, and we beheld his glory, the glory as of the only-begotten of the Father, full of grace and truth . . . (John 1.1–2, 14)

though it is likely that John's notion of the *Logos* had roots, less in Greek philosophy than in Jewish theology, of the word, *memra*, as the sacred presence of God, uttered in the Temple.

The Christology of the Councils

The *logos*, as a concept, belonged both to God, as his expression, and to the cosmos, as its meaning. The next step in realization comes at the beginning of the fourth century, and provokes the first of those councils, later to be called 'œcumenical', that is, concerned with the whole inhabited world, *oikoumene*, as the Romans, hubristically, referred to the Roman Empire. We have already reflected on the Christian doctrine of creation out of nothing, and how this suggests a fundamental divide between the uncreated God and the created universe. The idea of creation out of nothing can be traced back, as we saw, to the second century, but its radical implications took time to be appreciated. For what the doctrine of creation out of nothing radically entails is that there is no middle ground between the uncreated and the created. What, then, about the *Logos*, the Word of God? Does the *Logos* belong with the uncreated God, as uncreated; with the created universe, as part of creation; or is it merely some kind of metaphor for the engagement between God and the universe? Too much had been invested in the notion of *Logos* for the last mentioned to be satisfactory. But if the *Logos* is uncreated, does that not mean that there are two uncreated beings . . . two Gods?

So argued a learned priest of the diocese of Egypt, one Arius. According to him, the Christian belief in one God could only be safe-guarded by saying that the *Logos* was created out of nothing, maybe in a special way – the first, through whom everything else was created – but nonetheless created, and created out of nothing. The Pope of Alexandria, Alexander, sharply disagreed with his priest, and excom-municated him. For Alexander, if the *Logos* is not truly God, and so uncreated, then the Incarnate *Logos*, the Word made flesh, was a purely created being, and could not be the presence of the grace and mercy of the uncreated God.

Athanasios, Alexander's young deacon, and later his successor, took up the struggle against Arius in the decades after Alexander's death. The controversy blew up in the early 320s (most likely) and came to the attention of Constantine shortly after he became sole emperor in 324, with the defeat of his one-time colleague and co-emperor, Likinios. To settle this unwelcome dispute he called a council in 325 at the city of Nicaea in Asia Minor (possibly because of its equable climate). The council condemned Arius and produced a symbol of faith (called in the West a creed, after its initial word *credo*, I believe), which included the word *homoousios*, to characterize the relationship between the *Logos*, or the Son, as he was more commonly called now, and the Father: the use of *homoousios* meant there was unbroken continuity of being between the Father and the Son, everything the Father was the Son was, save for owing his being to him.

We have already seen how this became the foundation stone of the doctrine of the Trinity, but it had profound implications for the way Christians were to come to think about Christ. Christ could no longer be thought of as God reaching out to human kind through his *Logos*, which was an intermediary between God and man. In Christ, the stark contrast between God and man was bridged by one who was both. The Son of God became the Son of Man; it becomes more common now to speak, less of the *Logos*, than of the Son, or sometimes in a frequently used formula: the 'Word of God, and God', that is, the 'Word of God, [who is] God'. This Christ, the Council of Nicaea affirmed, is what it is to be God, yet he is other than the One he calls Father – and this is known in the Spirit.

But how could the uncreated God be juxtaposed immediately with created humanity? The first attempts to articulate this argued that God could not unite himself to a complete humanity – and that this was not necessary, for Christ had only to be human enough for God to make contact with humans. The most famous theologian to think like this was a friend of Athanasios and his supporter in the fight against what they called Arianism, which did not end with the Council of Nicaea in 325 but lasted in one form or another for the next 50 years. His name was Apollinaris, and he was bishop of Laodicea (not the city of the Apocalypse, but a coastal town in Syria). He maintained that Christ could not have a human soul, or at least not a human mind; there could not be two centres of activity in Christ – one divine, one human – for this would destroy the unity of Christ, nor was it necessary, for all that was needed in the Incarnation was to bring the power of the divine into contact with frail humanity. If Christ's human mind could make up its own mind, as it were, then our salvation would be jeopardized.

This heresy, called Apollinarianism, was countered not least by St Gregory of Nazianzos, later called 'the Theologian', who argued that if the Word of God did not assume a human mind, then the human mind would not have been healed, but that it was precisely the human mind and will that stood in need of healing. As he put it: 'the unassumed is the unhealed'.[6] At the Œcumenical Council held at Constantinople in 381, Apollinarianism was condemned as a heresy. Indeed, at that council an attempt was made to define the lineaments of Orthodox Christianity, and measures set up to see that this Orthodoxy was enforced throughout the Empire.

Although heretical, the basic intuition of Apollinarianism was not completely wrong. His idea that in Christ the Word of God became a human being and lived a human life, and that, as the Word made flesh, there was a union between God and man: this was how most Christians were coming to formulate their belief. But what kind of unity would be possible for such a being? For most Christians the response was along these lines: this is a mystery beyond our

---

[6] Gregory Nazianzen, *Ep.* 101 [= *ep.* 1 *ad Cledonium*], 5 (English translation in: St Gregory of Nazianzus, *On God and Christ: The Five Theological Orations and Two Letters to Cledonius* [trans. Frederick Williams and Lionel Wickham; Crestwood, NY: St Vladimir's Seminary Press, 2002], 158).

understanding; there are various analogies we can draw, but the truth escapes our comprehension. Yet there must be real unity. It is evident from the Gospels that the Lord was a single being, not two beings inhabiting the same skin. One way of putting this unity was to say that there was in Christ one centre of activity: whatever Christ did could be said to be what the Word who had assumed the humanity was doing, there was no one else there to be the subject of Christ's activity, and yet everything the Word did in Christ was done through the humanity of Christ; the Word as Christ did not operate independently.

There was, however, a group of theologians in Antioch who found this model unsatisfactory, and in interpreting the Gospel accounts of Christ wanted to distinguish between two 'persons', perhaps characters. Some acts of Christ could be ascribed to the Word – his works of miracles, for instance; others had to be ascribed to the human person in Christ – his being hungry and thirsty, and other manifestations of human need. The controversy became a conflict when one of these theologians, Nestorios, was appointed to the increasingly important see of Constantinople, the capital of the Roman Empire, 'New Rome'. The flashpoint was the title for the Virgin Mary of *Theotokos*, the 'one who gave birth to God'. Cyril of Alexandria, who took up the struggle against Nestorios, maintained that to deny this title, or even qualify its use, amounted to a denial of the Incarnation, according to which the one to whom Mary gave birth was indeed God Incarnate, God with us, Emmanuel.

At a council held in Ephesos, the third Œcumenical Council, in 431, Nestorios was condemned and eventually deposed. His supporters were called Nestorians. After the council many of them left the Roman Empire and settled among the Persians; later some became missionaries and took the gospel as far as China.[7] In 433 Cyril agreed a 'Formula of Union' with Nestorios' more moderate supporters, in which it was affirmed that Christ was to be understood to be *homoousios* with the Father in his divinity, as had been asserted since Nicaea, but also *homoousios* with us in his humanity. The Son, who was 'one of the Trinity', in an expression that became increasingly popular, as incarnate 'in the flesh' became truly one of us.

---

[7] Cf. Andrew Louth, *Greek East and Latin West: The Church AD 681–1071* (Crestwood, NY: St Vladimir's Seminary Press, 2007), 24.

How did Cyril and his supporters (in reality most Christians, at least in the East) understand the attribution to Christ of both divine qualities, such as working miracles, and human qualities, like hunger and thirst? In principle it was very simple: it was precisely to bear our weaknesses and the damage done to humanity by our sinfulness that the Word took on flesh in the first place. If the Word made flesh did not bear the weaknesses and diminishments of the fallen human condition, but they were borne by some 'human person' alongside the Word, then the Incarnation would achieve nothing. It was precisely in his love for humanity that the Word or Son of God assumed a human nature and lived a human life, and in this way overcame the havoc we had brought on ourselves, and offered us the hope of living the divine life, becoming deified.

The acceptance of Ephesos in accordance with the 'Formula of Union' was not the end of the matter, however. After Cyril's death in 444, controversy began again. Some Christians felt that the unity of Christ was being compromised by the way the 'Formula of Union' was being interpreted, and felt furthermore that if the unity of Christ was compromised, then so was the hope of our salvation. The events surrounding Chalcedon, the next Œcumenical Council held in 451, are complex, but the result was a conciliar definition, or *horos*, in which it was affirmed that there is

> one and the same Christ, Son, Lord, only-begotten, acknowledged in two natures which undergo no confusion, no change, no division, no separation; at no point was the difference between the natures taken away through the union, but rather the property of both natures is preserved and comes together into a single person and a single subsistent being [*hypostasis*] . . .[8]

The Council of Chalcedon settled little; Christians in the East divided over whether they thought this definition correctly expressed Cyril's teaching or, on the contrary, betrayed it. The schism produced by this council has lasted to the present day; the whole family of Eastern Churches, nowadays called the Oriental Orthodox Churches, continue to reject Chalcedon. Nevertheless, in the Orthodox tradition, the Council of Chalcedon is regarded as the council that provided

---

[8] *Decrees of the Ecumenical Councils* (ed. Norman P. Tanner SJ; 2 vols; London: Sheed & Ward, 1990), I.86.

the fundamental answer as to who Christ is: in Christ, God assumed humanity, so as to be able to die, and deliver us from death. So we might say that at Chalcedon it was affirmed that Christ shows us what it is to be God in the way he dies as a human being.

Further reflection on Christ and his nature took its guidelines from the definition of the Council of Chalcedon. The succeeding, complex history is perhaps best regarded as a series of ways of preventing various misunderstandings as to who Christ is; indeed, this is perhaps the best way of understanding the achievement of the Œcumenical Councils as a whole.

In the sixth century reflection focused on seeking to avoid further misunderstanding about the unity of Christ. In particular, attempts were made to accommodate the conviction of those who had rejected Chalcedon that it was necessary to affirm that 'One of the Trinity suffered in the flesh': that the union of natures in Christ was so deep that suffering in some mysterious way entered into the Trinity itself, so that, whatever suffering we endure, we can be sure that this suffering has been in some way embraced by God himself – a doctrine sometimes called 'theopaschism'. But it did little to halt the growing schism in the East between the Orthodox and those the Orthodox called 'monophysites' (so-called because they believed in 'one nature in Christ').

The seventh century saw a serious political crisis for the Byzantine Empire in which it lost most of its eastern provinces, where the monophysites were strongest, first to the Persians, and then, after a brief respite, to Islam – in the event, for ever. This provoked a further attempt to achieve union over the understanding of Christ that we need briefly to look at, as it involves the reflections of one of the greatest Byzantine theologians, St Maximos the Confessor.

In probably the 620s, some theologians (including the Œcumenical Patriarch, Sergios) thought that agreement with the monophysites could be reached on the basis of Chalcedon by accepting that there was one divine person in Christ (the second person of the Trinity), in which were united the two natures, divine and human, but that, furthermore, there was only one activity (*energeia*) – a divine–human, or *theandric*, activity – in Christ. Everything Christ did was both human and divine; it was impossible to separate out his activities between the human and the divine. In itself it was a brilliant suggestion, but it met with mistrust from those committed to Chalcedon;

for one thing, it seemed to contradict the 'Formula of Union' of 433, which had been reaffirmed at Chalcedon. Further reflection followed and a refinement was suggested, according to which there was only one will in Christ, the divine will. It is not at all clear what was meant, whether Christ had no human will, or a quiescent one; but opposition to monothelitism was led by St Maximos the Confessor, and eventually triumphed at the sixth Œcumenical Council, held at Constantinople in 680–1. For Maximos the problem with mono-thelitism was the same as the problem with Apollinarianism: Christ's humanity would be defective. Furthermore it was the human will that had brought about the Fall, so the human will needed healing, and if Christ had no human will, then he could not heal it. Maximos quoted the remark of Gregory the Theologian: 'the unassumed is the unhealed'.

That is a brief sketch of the gradual clarification of Orthodox belief about Christ. All the way through, the concern was to preserve the unity in Christ of the divine nature with the human nature: the divine nature of the person he was, and the human nature that the person of Christ had assumed. The dangers were seen to be: either the Godhead of Christ was diminished in some way to make it accessible to contact with the human (this was the case with Arianism, and also with some forms of Gnosticism, and indeed some forms of the *logos* theology), or the humanity of Christ was incomplete, to make room for the Godhead, as it were, or the human and divine were held apart and achieved no proper unity. The Orthodox Church found in the definition of Chalcedon a way of holding to our con-viction that in Christ we encounter the Son, the second person of the Trinity, 'one of the Trinity', assuming a human nature and living a human life. As we sing at Vespers on the Feast of the Nativity:

Come, let us rejoice in the Lord as we tell of the present mystery. The middle wall of partition has been destroyed, the flaming sword turns back, the Cherubim withdraw from the tree of life; and I partake of the paradise of delight, from which I was cast out through dis-obedience. The undeviating image of the Father, the stamp of his eternity, takes the form of a servant, and without suffering change comes out from the Mother who knew no wedlock; what he was he remains, being true God, and what he was not he assumes, becoming man for the love of mankind. To him let us cry out: God, born of a Virgin, have mercy on us.

5

Sin, death and repentance

Repentance and Christ

We encounter Christ; we understand him to be God the Son, taking on human nature, so that he can be mortal and suffer death. In this encounter we come to recognize that all is not well with ourselves. At the end of Chapter 4, we recalled one of the hymns, or troparia, that we sing on the Feast of the Nativity of Christ: a hymn that contemplates the mystery of Christ, his becoming human 'for the love of mankind', and that reminds us of the paradise of delight for which we were intended and to which Christ restores us. As we encounter Christ, we encounter the mystery of repentance; we cry out in the final words of the troparion, 'Lord, have mercy!' What should be our reaction? Partly it is a reaction at the wonder of God, a reaction in which we are conscious of our creatureliness, our frailty. But there is more than that. Each one of us stands before God and each one of us realizes the ways in which we have fallen short of what we were created for, and the ways in which we have sinned. But it is not just our personal sin of which we are conscious; we are aware that in some way we belong to a world that has gone astray, to a society that is governed by values that are not true. We realize this, not as a way of excusing ourselves, but because it seems that we are caught up in a state of estrangement that is not simply of our making, though we have made it worse, that we belong to a fallen world, a world that falls short of what it was intended for.

Beauty and disorder

We can see this as we look at the world of creation. There we see a created order of beings both visible and invisible, a creation which, because created out of nothing, manifests nothing but God himself, for the whole created order is to be seen as a theophany, a manifestation of God, indeed a manifestation of God's beauty.

But as we look at the world in which we live, we realize that there is something else. There is, certainly, beauty – especially perhaps in nature: the beauty of mountains and forests, of rivers, lakes and oceans, of the living creatures that inhabit the created order, not least human beings themselves. There is beauty, too, in what creatures make of their environment: from nests and other dwelling places, to the buildings with which humans adorn their living space – both homes, and public buildings, and temples and churches – and what they put in them, furniture, decorations and so on. There is a further beauty in what we might call culture: arrangements of objects, tools and so on – some of which we find in species other than human beings – through to paintings, statues, carvings; music, both for the human voice and for instruments; and poems, stories and other forms of literature, where our ability to communicate goes beyond the utile and delights and intrigues our minds.

There are hints of this in the early chapters of Genesis: we read of Jabal 'the father of those who dwell in tents and have cattle' (Gen. 4.20), of Jubal 'the father of those who play on the lyre and pipe' (Gen. 4.21), Tubal-cain 'the forger of all instruments of bronze and iron' (Gen. 4.22). But the account in Genesis is part of a history that leads to the story of Noah, ushered in by the Lord's seeing 'that the wickedness of man was great in the earth, and that every imagination of his heart was only evil continually' (Gen. 6.5).

And this corresponds with what we see when we look at the created order. There is, as we have seen, beauty, but there is much that mars that beauty. Natural beauty is destroyed or obscured by human aggression. Furthermore, we humans do not just shape our environment by making ourselves at home in it; we build defensive settlements, make weapons with which to defend ourselves and wreak destruction on one another. Limited resources lead to inequality: there are those who oppress others and those who are oppressed. The Hebrew prophets are eloquent in their denunciation of such oppressive inequality:

> Woe to those who lie upon beds of ivory, and stretch themselves upon their couches, and eat lambs from the flock, and calves from the midst of the stall; who sing idle songs to the sound of the harp, and like David invent for themselves instruments of music, who drink wine in bowls, and anoint themselves with the finest oils, but are not grieved over the ruin of Joseph! (Amos 6.4–6)

Sexual differentiation and the love of man and woman can be both the source of one of the greatest of human delights, and the cause of the deepest heartbreak.

Human kind and the Fall

What went wrong? The Fathers mostly consider this question in their interpretation of the story of Adam and Eve and their sin in the Garden of Eden and expulsion from paradise into this world. I say 'mostly', because consideration of the story of Noah and his ark, and the Tower of Babel (or the 'Confusion of Tongues' in the Greek translation), also provoke reflection on the presence of evil in the world. But the story of Adam's fall is the archetypal account, mostly, I would suggest, because of the way the apostle Paul casts Christ as the 'Second Adam', come to remedy the effects of Adam's sin. If Christ is the 'second Adam' who comes to redeem us, then it is to the 'first' Adam that we are bound to look to find out what went wrong.

There are a number of preliminary observations that I want to make about Orthodox teaching on the Fall. As with the Fathers, it is presented as reflection on the story of Adam and Eve. It is in fact a matter of telling stories: stories that help to explain where we are now. Storytelling seems to be fundamental to how we humans come to understand ourselves; it is by telling stories and placing ourselves in them that we understand what it is to be human, and to be the humans that we are. This seems to be true from the earliest story-telling of which we know to the storytelling that we find nowadays in novels and films. Indeed, the stories we tell do not seem to advance much. They change in the way they are presented – from early accounts of heroes and gods to the complex layering of reflection that we find in a novel by Henry James, for instance – but the fundamental mythological patterns seem to be of great antiquity; we still turn to ancient Greek myths for these aboriginal myths.

I stress this, because there is a tradition of interpretation that gets very anxious about whether we are to take the stories in Genesis 'literally' or not. In the Fathers we find a way of interpretation that transcends these issues, or at least places them in another light. It seems to me perfectly clear that the Scriptures were read in a way that meant that they were neither taken at a simply literal level, nor at a level that dispensed altogether with a literal interpretation. If we have a problem with this, it is likely to be our problem.

A further problem is the way in which, for some reason that I am not at all clear about, we objectify, as it were, the notion of the 'Fall'. This is so much a part of how most Christians think of things that I sometimes find it difficult to convey what I mean. Put in a simple way, the Fathers simply do not talk about 'the Fall' as some objective event. The Greek noun for fall – *ptôsis* – seems rarely to be used to describe what happened to Adam.

It is, I think, significant, when you *do not* have a word for a thing. The Fathers seem to me (this is, I admit, a subjective impression) to talk about what Adam did: he sinned, he was disobedient, he turned away from God. The consequences were disastrous: the world of harmony that God had intended in creating the cosmos with the human central to it was destroyed. The principle of harmony was taken away; the elements that should have fitted together fell apart and became opposed to one another. We are hearing about a process, and furthermore hearing about this process from the perspective of another process, or perhaps a deeper process: God's continuing love for the world he created, and his continuing longing to lead the created order to the end for which he created it.

In treating the question of sin and death and destruction, it seems to me that the theology of the Fathers never lost sight of a more important consideration: that the world had been created to be a place where human beings, created in the image of God, would be able to draw close to God and bring into being a union of wills – a cooperation, a harmony – that amounts to something greater than anything that even God could fashion. Put another way, if what God wants is a loving union between himself and the beings that he has created, primarily the human beings he has made, then these beings need to learn to love. They cannot be created knowing what that means: it is something that comes from experience, either innocent experience or (as turned out to be the case) an experience that has to learn by its mistakes. God created human beings that needed to learn to love; he created a beginning that needed to move towards fulfilment.

That means that there is, as it were, an arc that passes from creation to deification, union with God. But humans did not pass along that arc, as intended; they departed from it. They introduced sin, death, destruction: a problem brought about by human misuse of free will, a problem that needs to be dealt with and leads to what one might think of as the lesser arc leading from fall to redemption. It is possible to become concerned with the lesser arc from fall to redemption to such an extent that one loses sight of the greater arc passing from creation to deification, but the theology of the Fathers – and Orthodox theology, when it is true to itself – avoids this danger, and never forgets that we are dealing with God's creation, created for union with him.

Another way of putting this is that it seems to be characteristic of Orthodox theology that it considers the question of Adam's sin and its consequences from the perspective of the resurrection of Christ. The icon, called 'The Resurrection', is not a picture of Christ rising from the tomb, that we are familiar with from Western art; rather, it is a depiction of Christ destroying the gates of hell and bringing out from hell, witnessed by King David and King Solomon and some of the prophets, our forefather and foremother, Adam and Eve, as the first of a crowd of people (whose heads sometimes stretch back into the caverns of hell), who are being brought out of hell by Christ's victory over death in the resurrection. In the Orthodox calendar, on the Sunday before Christmas we commemorate 'all those who were well-pleasing to God from Adam until Joseph the Betrothed of the most-holy Mother of God'. Adam 'well-pleasing to God'? Is not Adam the archetypal sinner? Maybe, but in the Orthodox tradition he is the archetypal penitent, too: we shall come back to that later. Adam is commemorated as he is now: one whose penitence made it possible for him to be redeemed from hell by Christ at his resurrection.

Death and sin

There is something else, too, that flows from looking back to the Fall from the perspective of the resurrection: the resurrection is seen as the conquest of Christ over *death*, and so it is death, rather than sin, that is central to the Orthodox understanding of the consequences of Adam's disobedience. In Genesis, it is indeed death that is the promised punishment for eating of the tree of the knowledge of good and evil (cf. Gen. 2.17), and it is the introduction of death into the world that is seen as the result of Adam's sin.

What that meant is treated by the Fathers in a host of ways that we cannot pursue in detail here, but they explore what it means for the world to come under the sway of death, rather than under the sway

70

of sin. Some see it as meaning that Adam (and Eve) would not have died, had they not sinned: not that they were created immortal, but that, like Enoch (Gen. 5.24), they would have been 'taken' in some way. Others see a change in the meaning of death; physical death would have come upon Adam, but it would have meant something different – perhaps on analogy with the way in which after Christ has conquered death in the resurrection, Christians still die, but not without hope. But what has been unleashed on the world by Adam's sin has been death.

This is depicted in a striking way in the early chapters of St Athanasios' *On the Incarnation*: Adam's disobedience leads to the introduction of death and corruption into the cosmos. Death and corruption, *thanatos* and *phthora*, stalk the pages of Athanasios' text like a couple of furies: the world created out of nothing is dissolving back into nothing.[1] The world under the sway of death is a world characterized by corruption, disintegration; it is a world in which it is impossible to achieve anything, where all human intentions are like building on sand – they are impermanent, fragile. In fact, it seems to me to be suggested that it is not so much sin that causes death, as death that causes sin, by sapping our determination, for nothing that we do has any permanence; it is all being carried away by the corruption that has been unleashed on the world. What, then, is the point?

Athanasios asks – like Anselm many centuries later: Could not Adam have repented of his sin? Anselm's reply, famously, was that repentance would have done nothing, or far too little, to mitigate the offence that he had committed against God by his disobedience. Athanasios' reply is rather different: repentance might have availed for Adam himself, but would have still left the cosmos in a state of devastation: as if Adam had taken away the coping stone of the central arch of a building, and brought the whole building down about his ears. Saying 'Sorry' would not be enough![2]

St Athanasios treats of the Fall at the beginning both of *On the Incarnation* and of the first part of that two-part work, *Against the Nations*. There he presents a somewhat different account, often treated as if it were a less satisfactory sketch, though I would take it rather as complementary. He sees human beings – rational beings, as he puts

---

[1] See *On the Incarnation* 3—6.
[2] See *On the Incarnation* 7; cf. Anselm, *Cur Deus homo* 20.

it – created to live in contemplation of God through the Word of God, and thus to 'rejoice and converse with God, living an idyllic and truly blessed and immortal life'. But these rational beings have turned away from contemplating God and turned – where? for they are created out of nothing – to themselves, and to the world that they fashion from . . . nothing. And so the soul comes to 'harbour fears and terrors and pleasures and thoughts of mortality'.[3] From contemplating God and living in a world of reality and life, Adam, or human kind, contemplates non-being and enters a haunted world of unreality and death – which Athanasios spells out as a world of immoral desires and longings, populated by the gods and goddesses of Greek paganism.

Adam and ancestral sin

In both scenarios, Adam had abandoned the world as God created it, and tried to fashion an imaginary world of his own devising, an unreal world, unstable and subject to corruption. Athanasios seems aware, too, that the first man is called Adam, because that is the word for 'man' in Hebrew:[4] with the suggestion that Adam is every one of us, rather than, or at least as much as, an historical figure.

But we need to pause and ask what kind of account this is. A mythical account of 'everyman', or an historical account of the first man? I have already suggested that this distinction would not, perhaps, have seemed to the Fathers quite as sharp as we are inclined to make it.

Mostly, it is the story of 'everyman'; it is a story that is true of each one of us: we have all turned away from God, we all inhabit the world of corruption and death. But there is more to it than that, for it is not as if we have each created our own world of death. It is rather that we seem to have been born into such a world. To account for this the Fathers conceive of sin as being more than simply personal sin. What they mean by this is that if I were able to look at the consequences of my sin, it would seem all so much more than I could really be blamed for. It is as if the consequences of sin are amplified, in the course of nature, as it were, in an alarming way; the consequences of my sin mingle with the consequences of others' sin and the whole combines to form a kind of deafening cacophony.

---

[3] *Against the Nations* 3.
[4] *Against the Nations* 2.

The Greek Fathers speak in this connexion of 'ancestral sin', *propaterikon amartema*, sin of our forefathers, inherited sin. We are born into a ruined cosmos, ruined at a moral, rather than a physical level (though there are areas – disease, for instance – where it is difficult to draw a line); we add our bit to the devastation, but most of it was already laid waste long before we came along. The story of Adam speaks of the very beginning of this process, but just as we are implicated in a sin that is bigger than we are, so, too, Adam has unleashed consequences of sin that are more than he could be regarded as personally responsible for.

In the West, with Augustine and his followers, there develops a notion of original sin, *peccatum originale*: a sin that has its origin in Adam and infects, like an inherited disease, all humanity. This idea, in this very specific sense, never developed in the East, mostly, I suppose, because it seemed that the notion of ancestral sin explained well enough the way in which the effects of sin are more than merely personal. It also seems to me that the notion of ancestral sin tends to see the story of Adam and Eve as typical, rather than needing it to be strictly historical, though, as I have said, for the Fathers this distinction was not drawn very sharply. It might, however, affect how we today interpret Genesis 3.

Sin and the cosmos

We need to go a little further here, because there is one aspect of the story of Adam and Eve that can cause problems. The story of the Fall presents a human story that implicated the whole cosmos. The Fathers developed this notion by drawing on ideas in some of the classical philosophers – especially Plato and the Stoics – about the relationship of the human and the cosmic. We shall discuss this in greater detail in Chapter 6, but we need to introduce it now in outline.

Many philosophers saw a relationship between the human and the cosmic. The human was regarded as a microcosm, a little cosmos, in which all the structures of the cosmos were reflected; similarly, the cosmos could be regarded as the human writ large. Christian theologians worked this notion into their idea, drawn from Genesis, of the human created in the image of God. As God's image, the human had been set at the heart of the cosmos with the role of holding the whole cosmos together. When Adam and Eve relinquished their role as bond of the cosmos – *syndesmos tou kosmou* – the cosmos lost much of its harmony; the harmony of the stars and planets was preserved, though perhaps it became obscure to man, but the harmony that had existed in paradise between humans and animals, for instance, was destroyed (only to be glimpsed in ascetics like St Antony or St Jerome, in whose lives some aspects of the original paradisal harmony could be found – friendly lions, for instance).

If you believe, as Genesis sets out, that the cosmos was created in six days (however these 'days' are understood) with the human coming at the end as the crown of creation, then this picture looks imaginatively plausible. If, however, one believes that the universe is as modern science thinks of it – an almost immeasurably long development from some primitive 'big bang', through the evolution of stars and galaxies, with human life emerging almost as an afterthought – it seems quite unimaginable. How could the cosmos depend on creatures that have only existed for an almost infinitesimal time at the end, on a smallish planet, circling a moderate sized star, in a fairly insignificant galaxy? Such considerations will occupy us from time to time in succeeding chapters, but here there is something more immediate.

Most scientists think that human life has evolved from earlier forms of life, and shares a great deal with other forms of animal life that have evolved alongside the human. Evolution is understood as a process measured not in years, or centuries, but millennia – with human beings emerging, alongside other forms of animal life, towards the end, not so very long ago in terms even of geological time, let alone cosmic time. Do Christians have to believe that Adam and Eve existed, and that they sinned, and that their sin has infected all subsequent human beings? Do we have to believe that there was an original couple, that *homo sapiens* emerged from some kind of *homo erectus* as a single couple, in a particular place, and if so where? There are, as we know, Christians who believe this, and indeed not a few of them are Orthodox Christians. I do not, however, think we, as Orthodox, need to commit ourselves to such a position, and I want briefly to explain why.

Ancestral sin and evolution

First, however, we need to grasp why Darwin and the theory of evolution caused such controversy among Christians from the nineteenth century onwards, though it is worth remembering that not all Christians felt challenged in this way; many of them fell on the idea of evolution as a wonderful explanation of the place of the human in the cosmos – notable among these were Russian Orthodox philosophers such as Vladimir Solov'ev. Darwin caused controversy, not merely because his ideas contradicted Genesis, but because they fell foul of the way in which Genesis had been read by those influenced by the Enlightenment, for it was the Enlightenment that conceived of the human as almost exclusively rational and intellectual, and set the human at a distance from the animal.

When the Fathers interpret Genesis, they see the human as sharing a very great deal with animal, and indeed plant-like, creation. The possession of reason, the gift of being in the image of God, makes the human distinctive, indeed raises the human to a position that transcends the animal and the plant-like, both as being nobler, and also as bearing responsibility for the rest of creation, but the human still shares a very great deal with the rest of creation, both animal and plant-like, and even with the inanimate creation. St Gregory of Nyssa, the younger brother of St Basil the Great, discussed the nature of the human in his work, *On the Creation of the Human*,[5] which he wrote to supplement his brother's set of homilies on the Six Days of Creation, the *Hexaemeron*, as presented in Genesis. Basil's homilies are incomplete, for reasons unknown: the creation of man is only mentioned, not discussed.

In his work, Gregory deals at some length with the nature of the human. His account draws on the accepted philosophical ideas of his day, not least Aristotle's analysis of the human make-up. At one point, Gregory tackles the idea that the human being has a soul that shares a great deal with the soul we find in animals, and indeed the soul we find in plants: the Greek word for soul, *psyche*, means 'life', and so the word soul suggests the principle of the life that any living being has. So the human may be said to have an animal soul and a plant-like soul, as well as a rational or intellectual soul. Yet a human being does not have three souls, rather the intellectual soul manifests itself at the

---

[5] Alas, no modern English translation of this has been published. Two rather different homilies, either the last two homilies of Basil's *Hexaemeron* or written to supply them (maybe by Gregory of Nyssa), have been translated by Nonna Verna Harrison in: St Basil the Great, *On the Human Condition* (Crestwood, NY: St Vladimir's Seminary Press, 2005).

animal and plant-like level, which the human shares with animals and plants. What is meant to happen with humans is that the intellectual soul expresses itself through, and makes use of, the lower levels, the animal and plant-like. But the Fall, as we have seen, has disturbed the harmony of God's creation, and this is true at what one might call the psychological level: instead of expressing itself through the animal and plant-like, the intellect finds itself serving the animal drives and plant-like needs (for nourishment, for example), and producing what we call bestial behaviour – which is really something distinctively human, though not anything to be proud of. So the human has two aspects – one reaching towards the divine, the other succumbing to the animal – and is in fact poised on a watershed between affinity to the divine and affinity to lower creation. Gregory puts it like this:

> It seems to me that the human bears two contradictory likenesses – shaped in the divine aspect of his mind after the divine beauty, but also bearing, in the passionate impulses that arise in him, a likeness to the bestial nature. Frequently his reason is reduced to bestiality, and obscures the better element by the worse through its inclination and disposition towards the animal. For whenever anyone drags down the activity of thought to these, and forces reason to become the servant of the passions, there occurs a sort of distortion of the good character towards the irrational image, his whole nature being refashioned in accordance with this, as reason cultivates the new shoots of the passions, and little by little causes them to grow into a multitude; for once [reason] makes common cause with passion, it produces a thick and diverse crop of evils.
>
> Thus our love of pleasure took its beginning from our likeness to the irrational creation, but was increased by human transgressions, begetting such a variety of sinning flowing from pleasure, as is not to be found among the animals. Thus the rising of anger is indeed akin to the impulse of the animals, but it is increased by the alliance with our processes of thought. For thence come resentment, envy, deceit, conspiracy, hypocrisy: all these are the result of the evil husbandry of the intellect. For if the passion is stripped of this alliance with the processes of thought, the anger that is left behind is short-lived and feeble – like a bubble, bursting as soon as it comes into being. Thus the gluttony of pigs introduces covetousness, and the high spirit of the horse becomes the origin of pride; and everything that proceeds from the lack of reason in animal nature becomes vice by the wicked use of the intellect.

So, therefore, on the contrary, if reason instead assumes sway over such emotions, each of them is transmuted into a form of virtue. For anger produces courage, cowardice caution, fear obedience, hatred aversion from vice, the power of love the desire for what is truly beautiful. High spirit in our character raises our thought above the passions, and keeps it from bondage to what is base. The great apostle, too, praises such a form of mental elevation when he bids us constantly to 'set our minds on things that are above' (Col. 3.2) and so we find that every such motion, when elevated by loftiness of mind, is conformed to the beauty after the divine image.[6]

This is very much more subtle than – quite unfairly – attributing the worse characteristics of the human to animals; rather, the human shares a great deal with the animal world, but makes it human either by raising it to something that furthers our own assimilation to God, our own process of deification, or by embroidering and developing it in characteristically human ways, fashioning vices that take their cue from innocent animal patterns of behaviour. But my immediate point is simply that such a view of what it is to be human acknowledges that there is a great deal in our humanity that we share with the animal world. Gregory himself had no notion of evolution – it would be completely anachronistic to suppose that he did – but, with his conception of the human, the notion that our evolutionary past manifests a great deal of commonality with the animal world would not have seemed inconceivable or in any way a diminishment of what it is to be human.

My first point, then, is that the idea of continuity between the animal and the human presupposed by the theory of evolution is not at all at odds with how the Fathers understood human nature. Orthodox theology should not have any problem at such a level.

What about Adam and Eve as the original human couple? Here I would draw a distinction between the notions of ancestral sin, found in the Greek Fathers and accepted by Orthodox theology, and of original sin, characteristic of much Western theology, under the influence of Augustine. Original sin involves the idea of some baneful inheritance from Adam (and strictly speaking in Augustinian theology that we are each, individually, responsible for Adam's sin and justly

---

[6] Gregory of Nyssa, *On the Creation of the Human* 18. 3–5 (my translation).

punished for it). It may well be possible to recast this doctrine in some form that dispenses with the historicity of Adam, but clearly there is work to be done.

With the notion of ancestral sin, the situation seems to me rather different. What is being affirmed is that something of the sinful condition in which we find ourselves is inherited from our forefathers and foremothers, who are in some way represented by Adam and Eve. It is not claimed that we are *responsible* for ancestral sin, simply that we are affected by it. The world into which we are born is affected by the sin of our forebears: the harmony God intended in creating the world has been shattered, the moral atmosphere in which we grow up poisoned, for we are not isolated individuals, but enter into our humanity at a moral level through interaction with the members of our family, and the society in which we live; in a fallen world these nurturing communities are affected by sinful presuppositions, our ideals are often shallow, our trust in our fellow human beings damaged and weakened. I do not think it necessary to pretend that we know enough about the emergence of humanity in the evolutionary process to be definite about an original couple; simply that as human beings found themselves growing in awareness of something beyond the merely human, manifest in the way in which the first signs of humanity in the archaeological record begin to include some awareness of a divine transcendence – signs pointing beyond the everyday, that the surviving evidence prevents us from defining with much clarity – they found, as we do, that the pull of more evident pleasure, or a sense of the self expressing itself in aggression towards the other, was too great to resist. Here, as elsewhere, there is much that we do not understand, and we need not pretend to any greater clarity than we can discern.

Adam and Eve . . . and repentance

The figures of Adam and Eve are, nonetheless, powerful, but powerful as inclusive figures that tell us about our own experience of evil and our own struggles towards repentance. The moment in the Orthodox Calendar when Adam becomes the focus of attention is the Sunday on which we commemorate Adam's expulsion from paradise, the day before Clean Monday, and therefore on the very threshold of Lent. In the first verse, or troparion, at Vespers we say:

78

The Lord my Creator, taking dust from the earth, formed me into a living creature, breathing into me the breath of life and giving me a soul; He honoured me as ruler on earth over all things visible, making me a companion of the angels. But Satan the deceiver, using the serpent as his instrument, enticed me by food, parted me from the glory of God and gave me over to the earth and the lowest depths of death. But, as Master and compassionate, call me back again.[7]

Adam laments his sin, and his expulsion from paradise, but ends calling out to God to call him back. Here is Adam as everyman; as we sing this verse we take it upon our lips and utter it from our heart. Like Adam, we were created; like Adam we have fallen; like Adam we call on God to call us back to himself. As the services continue, these themes are developed. Adam looks back to paradise and addresses it:

O precious paradise, unsurpassed in beauty, tabernacle built by God, unending gladness and delight, glory of the righteous, joy of the prophets, and dwelling of the saints, with the sound of your leaves pray to the Maker of all: may He open to me the gates which I closed by my transgression, and may He count me worthy to partake of the Tree of Life and of the joy which was mine when I dwelt in you beforehand.[8]

The next troparion reflects on this:

Adam was banished from paradise through disobedience and cast out from delight, beguiled by the words of a woman. Naked he sat outside the garden, lamenting 'Woe is me!' Therefore let us all make haste to accept the season of the Fast, obeying the traditions of the Gospel, that we may in all things be well pleasing to Christ and receive once more a dwelling-place in paradise.[9]

We all sit naked outside paradise with Adam, and lament; the season of the Great Fast we are about to embark on gives us the chance to share in Adam's penitence, so that we may find ourselves, with him, on the eve of Easter, grasped by the hand of the risen Christ and taken from banishment to paradise.

Adam laments, but does not despair. Even though naked and shut out of paradise he turns back to God in sorrow and repentance.

---

[7] Translations from the Greek Triodion, based on those in *The Lenten Triodion* (trans. Mother Maria and Archimandrite Kallistos Ware; London: Faber, 1978), 168.
[8] *The Lenten Triodion*, 169.
[9] *The Lenten Triodion*, 169.

I lament, I groan, I weep as I look upon the cherubim with the sword of fire set to guard the gate of Eden against all transgressors. Woe is me! I cannot enter unless You, O Saviour, grant me unhindered approach.

O Christ, my Saviour, boldly I put my trust in the abundance of your mercies and in the blood that flowed from your divine side; for through your blood you sanctified the nature of mortal man, O loving Lord, and opened to those that worship you the gates of paradise that of old were closed to Adam.[10]

The gates of paradise are a recurrent theme, and pick up a verse we have been singing at Matins on the Sundays before Lent, and continue to sing throughout Lent:

Open to me, O Giver of Life, the gates of repentance: for early in the morning my spirit seeks your holy temple, bearing a temple of the body all defiled. But as you are compassionate, cleanse it by your loving-kindness and mercy.[11]

In the last century, a monk of the Holy Mountain, the Russian peasant who is now known to the world as St Silouan, wrote a meditation on Adam called 'Adam's Lament'.[12] He begins by speaking of 'Adam, the father of mankind' and sees the worst consequences of Adam's sin and banishment from paradise in the fact that he was 'widowed of the love of God'; as a result, 'he suffered grievously and lamented with a great moan'. Adam, for St Silouan, is both an individual – now in paradise again – and a representative figure: representative of 'the soul which has known God through the Holy Spirit but has afterwards lost grace [and] experiences the torment that Adam suffered . . . [the] aching and deep regret in the soul that has grieved the beloved Lord'.[13]

So the story of Adam is, for St Silouan, the story of love lost, the loss regretted and the love eventually regained: human love for God, because God's love for us is constant, and unceasingly calls human beings back to him. One of the most poignant moments in the story

---

[10] *The Lenten Triodion*, 177.
[11] *The Lenten Triodion*, 101.
[12] First published in English by Fr Sofrony, his disciple, in a book called *The Undistorted Image: Staretz Silouan 1866–1938* (London: Faith Press, 1958), 137–44; now in the expanded English version, *Saint Silouan the Athonite* (Essex: Patriarchal and Stavropegic Monastery of St John the Baptist, 1991), 448–56.
[13] *Saint Silouan the Athonite*, 448.

of the Fall as Genesis relates it occurs when Adam realizes what he has done, discovers that he and Eve are naked, and they make for themselves aprons of fig leaves. 'And they heard the voice of the Lord God walking in the garden in the cool of the day, and the man and his wife hid themselves from the presence of the Lord God among the trees of the garden' (Gen. 3.8). They had walked with God in the garden in the time of their innocence, but now they hid themselves: their easy, unselfconscious intercourse with God was lost; their love for God had fled, they were afraid, and hid themselves.

It is that lost love that, for St Silouan, is the main consequence of Adam's sin; and it is the restoration of that love that God seeks from then on. The expulsion from paradise, the nakedness, the toil needed to support themselves, even the pain of childbirth, are seen as ways in which God seeks to stir man's conscience and bring him back to love. In 'Adam's Lament', St Silouan explores the plight of Adam – the plight of each one of us – and he ends with us humans calling on Adam to help us, to show us the way back. But Adam is silent, and when he speaks it is only to say: 'My children, leave me in peace. I cannot wrench myself from the love of God to speak to you . . . Trouble me not. I see the Mother of God in glory . . .'[14] It seems bafflingly heartless. But in St Silouan's account we humans go on pestering Adam, and he replies:

> Repent before the Lord, and entreat him. He loves man and will give all things . . . Greet tribulation. Wear down your bodies. Humble yourselves and love your enemies, that the Holy Spirit may take up His abode in you . . .[15]

Adam is unwilling to be mediator for his children; it is the second Adam who is that. He is unwilling even to be intercessor; we have the Mother of God and the saints. He tells us simply to repent, to go on knocking on the gates of repentance. 'Adam's Lament' ends:

> Adam lost the earthly paradise and sought it weeping. But the Lord through His love on the cross gave Adam another paradise, fairer than the old – a paradise in heaven where shines the Light of the Holy Trinity.[16]

---

[14] *Saint Silouan the Athonite*, 452–3.
[15] *Saint Silouan the Athonite*, 455–6.
[16] *Saint Silouan the Athonite*, 456.

6

Being human – being in the image of God

The doctrine of the image of God

Absolutely central to the way in which the Fathers understand the nature of humanity is the notion that human beings are created in the image and likeness of God. This doctrine is central not only to the Fathers' understanding of human nature, but also to their theology as a whole. In a little-known article, written over half a century ago, the Dominican theologian, Père Camelot, remarked:

> Now this theme of the image is, in the theology of the Fathers, above all the Greek Fathers, truly central: there one sees at the same time the meeting of Christology and Trinitarian theology, of anthropology and psychology, of the theology of creation and that of grace, of the problem of nature and the supernatural, the mystery of divinization, the theology of the spiritual life, the laws of its development and of its progress.[1]

The foundation of the doctrine of the image is to be found in the creation narrative of Genesis. There we read:

> And God said, Let us make human kind according to our image and according to our likeness; and let them rule over the fish of the sea and the birds of the air and the cattle and all the earth and all the creeping things that creep upon the earth. And God made human kind, according to his image God made him; male and female he made them. And God blessed them, and said, Increase and multiply and fill the earth and rule over it . . .   (Gen. 1.26–28a)

However, in the rest of the Bible little is made of this doctrine. In chapter 5 of Genesis, the events of the creation of man are summarized: 'In the day that God made Adam, he made him in the image of God;

---

[1] Th. Camelot OP, 'La théologie de l'image de Dieu', *Revue des Sciences philosophiques et théologiques* XL (1956), 443–71; here 443–4.

male and female he made them, and he blessed them' (Gen. 5.1–2). In the next verse, we are told that 'Adam begat a child according to his form and according to his image; and he named his name Seth'. Thereafter, there is no mention of the doctrine of the image until the Wisdom literature, where we read that God 'made [human kind] an image of his own self [or eternity]' (Wisd. 2.23) and that God 'made them according to his image' (Sir. 17.3). Wisdom itself is said to be 'an image of his goodness' (Wisd. 7.26).

In the New Testament we are told that man (not woman) is 'the image and glory of God' (1 Cor. 11.7), but it is Christ, too, who is said to be the image of God (2 Cor. 4.4; Col. 1.15). Language of the image is used of our relationship to Christ: we are to be 'conformed to the image of his Son' (Rom. 8.29); in 1 Corinthians it is said that 'just as we have borne the image of the earthly, so we shall bear the image of the heavenly' (1 Cor. 15.49), and in 2 Corinthians that 'we all, reflecting with unveiled face the glory of the Lord, are being changed into the same image from glory to glory' (2 Cor. 3.18). Colossians, too, speaks of our being 'clothed with the new [man] who is being renewed in knowledge according to the image of him who created him' (Col. 3.20): which is not entirely clear, but certainly sees the new creation as the restoration of the image in man.

The image of God in the Fathers

That may not seem very much, but the influence of ideas may be less in accordance with their frequency than with their resonance. And the notion that human kind was created according to the image of God found an enormous resonance in the hearts and minds of the Fathers.

There seem to me to be several converging reasons for this. First of all, the importance, that we have already seen, of the doctrine of creation. We are what we are, because God created us. He created us out of nothing; everything that we are is from God. Then, as many of the Fathers remark, there seems to be something special about the creation of human kind: for the rest of creation, God simply said, let something happen – 'Let there be light', and so on – but in the case of human kind, God seems to consider: 'Let us make human kind . . .' in verse 26 and then in the next verse, 'And God made human kind . . .' There seems some special act of deliberation about the creation of

83

human kind. Not only that, the human is made 'according to [God's] image, according to [his] likeness': being in God's image and likeness is at the heart of what it is to be human – the human is 'according to his image', he is like God in some way, he reflects in who he is something of what God is.

The Greek Fathers read Genesis in Greek – I have been careful to quote from the Greek Septuagint – and the Greek, to an educated ear, makes two further suggestions. First, 'according to the image', *kat' eikona*: *kata* is quite a strong preposition; it would suggest the question, 'According to what image?' The English 'in the image' just suggests that man was created as the image of God; the Greek raises the possibility of something more complex: man created according to the image of God. Who is? The New Testament suggests Christ, the image of God, the one who images forth God in his incarnate state. So maybe there is here, for the Christian Greek ear, the idea that human kind was created according to Christ, who is the image of the Father. This may remind one of the depiction of creation in the north portal of Chartres Cathedral, where the cruciform halo makes it evident that it is Christ who is the Creator (as the Nicene Creed affirms: 'through whom [that is, the Son] all things were made'), and in making man he makes one who is like him, who is in accordance with – *kata* – him. So our very creation entails a relationship, not just to God as Creator, but to Christ, the Son of God Incarnate.

But there is another point to note: verse 26 adds – 'and according to likeness'. The word translated 'likeness', *homoiosis*, suggests something more precise in Greek: the ending, *-osis*, implies a process, not a state (the Greek for likeness as a state would be *homoioma*). The word *homoiosis* would moreover have very definite resonances for anyone who had read Plato, who envisages the goal of the human life as *homoiosis* – likening, assimilation – to the divine. In the *Theaetetus*, Socrates remarks, in a phrase very popular among some of the Fathers: 'flight [from the world] is assimilation to God so far as is possible' (*Theat.* 176a). So, to be created according to the image of God and according to his likeness suggests that we have been created with some kind of affinity for God which makes possible a process of assimilation to God, which is, presumably, the point of human existence.

This idea chimes in very well with the few uses of the language of image in the New Testament, for it is in the context of saying something about the goal of our being disciples of Christ, that the New

Testament resorts to such language: we are being changed into his image from glory to glory. Even without using the language of image, there are passages in the New Testament that suggest much the same idea: for instance, in the first epistle of John we read, 'Beloved, we are God's children now; it does not yet appear what we shall be, but we know that when he appears we shall be like him, for we shall see him as he is' (1 John 3.2). The language of image is the language of sight; the suggestion of these passages is that being in the image means there is a likeness between human kind and God that enables us to see, to know, God – it is a kind of epistemological principle of much ancient philosophy that only 'like knows like': to know something is to discover an affinity. It suggests what I would call a contemplative understanding of what it is to be human, though there is nothing new in that – both Plato and Aristotle thought the same, and something similar is implied in Isaias' vision of the Lord in the Temple in Isaiah 6.

What then is it to be in the image of God? Often enough, we find the Fathers giving an answer in terms of human qualities, and these turn out to be qualities of the soul. 'The "according to the image"', says John Damascene, 'is manifest in intelligence [*noeron*] and free will [*autexousion*]'.[2] Being in the image means being a rational, or intelligent, being with free will. Sometimes the answer is more complex. Athanasios, for instance, talks about God's creating us and our being 'given something more':

> creating human beings not simply like all the irrational animals upon the earth, but making them according to his own image, and giving them a share of the power of his own Word, so that having as it were shadows of the Word and being made rational, they might be able to abide in blessedness, living the true life, which is really that of the holy ones in paradise.[3]

Being in the image, however, is not, for Athanasios, simply a matter of being rational, for otherwise the angels would be in the image, too, something that he denies:[4] being in the image is a gift to humanity, body and soul, which grants rationality to the human, but must mean

---

[2] *On the Orthodox Faith* 26 (my translation). There is a translation of this work in St John of Damascus, *Writings* (trans. Frederic H. Chase Jr; Fathers of the Church, 37; New York: Catholic University of America Press, 1958).

[3] *On the Incarnation* 3.

[4] *On the Incarnation* 13.

more than this. The more is, I think, for Athanasios, tied up with the fact that the image of God is Christ, the Word of God, whom we cannot understand apart from the Incarnation. It is in some way according to the image of God, understood as the Word of God Incarnate, that human kind was fashioned. This more complex notion unfolds in two ways.

Image and *logos*

First, we need to remember that it was in Greek that these ideas were thought through, and that something of what is meant is lost in translation, whether into Latin or into English. For the key word here is *logos*, which can be translated (as we have already seen) as word, or reason, or meaning, or principle; and the word translated 'rational' is, in Greek, *logikos*. So the translation 'rational' only preserves part of the meaning of the Greek *logikos*, and disguises the link the Greek suggests between the Word, or *Logos*, and *logikos*. The word *logikos* suggests, as its root meaning, participating in the *Logos*, or Word; it implies a relationship, rather than simply a property. And there is a parallel to be found here between the relationship *logikos–Logos* and the relationship 'being according to the image'–Image, *kat' eikona–Eikon*. In passing, it is striking that what is rather a clumsy expression in English, 'that which is according to the image', *to kat' eikona*, is a common term in Byzantine Greek, as, for instance, in the apolytikion for St Mary of Egypt, where we sing

> In you, Mother, was preserved unimpaired that which is according to
> the image (*to kat' eikona*); for you took up the cross and followed
> Christ, and by your deeds you have taught us to despise the flesh, for
> it passes away, but to care for the soul, which is a thing immortal. And
> therefore your spirit, holy Mary, rejoices with the Angels.[5]

What I am arguing is that limiting being in the image of God to being rational and possessing free will falls short in two respects of what the Greek Fathers generally mean by being according to God's image. First, being *logikos* means more than simply being rational; it means participating in the *Logos*, the Word, of God, including rationality, certainly, but also a capacity for recognizing and conveying

---

[5] *An Orthodox Prayer Book* (Eng. trans. Archimandrite Ephrem Lash; Milton under Wychwood: Fellowship of St Alban & St Sergius, 2009), 108.

meaning, for communicating, with one another and with God, and ultimately an affinity with God, that enables us to know him. Second, possessing *to kat' eikona* means having a relationship to God through his image, that is, the Word; it is not just a property or a quality, but a capacity for a relationship, a relationship that is fulfilled in attainment of *to kath'omoiosin*, being according to the likeness, assimilation with God.

To think of the human as 'according to the image' in this sense sets up a pattern: we have been created by God the Father in the image of the Word through the Word, so that, through the Word who created us we might come to the knowledge of God the Father – this whole process takes place by grace, that is, through the Spirit.

Image and Christ

My second point is a development of this. To be human is to be in the image, and being in the image, according to the image, entails a relationship to Christ, who is the image. Certainly he is an image in virtue of being the Word of God, the *Logos*, God's self-manifestation; but this is something we only fully understand through the Incarnation. Human kind is created according to an image – the Word of God – that we only truly know through the Incarnation. It is only through the Incarnation that we can truly understand what it is to be human. This is the main reason why I have kept back reflection on what it is to be human until this relatively late point in the book, for it is only in the light of Christ that we can grasp what is truly meant by being human. And the Fall only reinforces this. What we know from our experience of being human is what it is to be fallen humanity, but to be in the image is, at the very least, to bear some trace of true humanity, unfallen humanity, and it is unfallen humanity that we see in Christ. For the Word of God, in becoming man, became what we were meant to be. To be human is to have a nature with capacities, faculties, that are never properly realized in our fallen state; we have a glimpse of these faculties in Christ.

There is an illustration of what this might mean in an essay, recently translated, by Fr Sergii Bulgakov on the Gospel miracles.[6]

---

[6] Sergius Bulgakov, *Relics and Miracles: Two Theological Essays* (trans. Boris Jakim; Grand Rapids, MI: Eerdmans, 2011).

There he argues convincingly that it is a mistake to see the miracles as simply evidence of Christ's divinity (though that is the way in which they are taken by the Fathers, as a rule). They are evidence of the potentialities of the human, cooperating with divine grace:

> In their content miracles are works of love and mercy; in their significance they are manifestations of human power in the world, human power that is reinforced and illuminated by God's power . . . These tasks are *human* tasks, and these works are *human* works; and all of them are accessible to man, are assigned to him as a natural being, who at the same time is placed by God as the lord of creation and endowed with the gift of compassionate human love for man and for all creatures . . . It is true that not all of them are capable of being accomplished by human powers. Man is not yet able to eliminate death by natural means and to awaken people from the swoon of death, although he is approaching this; nor has he yet eliminated hunger, although he is seeking means to do so, and all this is something that does not surpass human powers. The proof of this is that all of Christ's miracles, in their content, could have been worked by divinely inspired saintly men, strengthened by God's grace; and consequently these miracles belong to the category of human power, to the category of man's lordship over the world, given by God to man at his creation.[7]

To sum up: being in the image certainly entails being rational and free, but that is not what it *means*; what being in the image means is having an affinity with God, not a natural affinity, but one granted us through God's grace, in virtue of which affinity we can know God, have some kind of communion with him. Put more exactly, I would say that being in the image of God means being able to pray. One of the aspects of the language of images is that images are not just likenesses or pictures, but that they are derived from an original. An image of God is derived from God, it manifests him as a kind of theophany, and the purpose of an image is to enable others to recognize the original, to draw them to the original. If one understands image in this sense, then the whole of St John's Gospel is concerned with the image: the Son imaging forth the Father, so that Christ can say to Philip, 'He who has seen me has seen the Father' (John 14.9).

The way in which images are essential to our understanding of – well, almost anything – is something that we shall pursue further in

---

[7] Bulgakov, *Relics and Miracles*, 78–9.

Chapter 7, when we think about the place of icons. Now I want to follow some other paths. But before I leave our consideration of being in the image, I want to add one further reflection. We have already seen the way in which the doctrine of creation out of nothing by God entails that, whatever havoc we humans have inflicted on the created order, the *logoi*, the 'deep structures', as we might think of them, of creation remain inviolable. One of the most moving moments in the biblical account of the Fall occurs after the eating of the apple: 'And they heard the voice of the Lord God walking in the garden in the cool of the day, and Adam and his wife hid themselves from the presence of the Lord God among the trees of the garden' (Gen. 3.8). Part of what it was to be human was the natural converse with God who walked in the garden with the human couple. It is that natural converse with God that we seek in prayer; it is that natural converse with God that has been restored by Christ's paschal mystery, that *parrhesia*, somewhat over-translated as 'boldness' in the words with which the priest invites the people to pray the Lord's Prayer in the liturgy: 'And count us worthy, Master, with boldness and without condemnation to dare to call upon you the God of heaven, as Father, and to say . . .'

Person and community

'And God made man, according to the image of God he made him; male and female he made them' (Gen. 1.27). I have abandoned gender-inclusive language, because the word translated 'man' here, *anthropos*, is not an abstract noun, like 'human kind', but a concrete noun: man (male or female). In the first part of the sentence we are told God made man in the singular, but in the last clause we are told that he made 'them' male and female. It is hardly a mistake. We are being told about the unity of humanity, and yet, that humanity is also a manifold, based on the distinction between the sexes, between male and female. This combination of one and many comes again in the next chapter when God makes woman from man's side, for 'it is not good for man to be alone' (Gen. 2.18), and presents her to him, saying that he should cleave to her, and 'the two will become one flesh' (2.24). 'One is one, and all alone, and ever more shall be so', as the folk song has it: not a good idea! The Scriptures present humanity as one-in-many, a unity embracing different persons.

In the New Testament, similar ideas are introduced. We are all, as baptized Christians, members of Christ, forming one body, the body of Christ. The apostle Paul presents a picture of the Church, consisting of many members, who are all bound up with one another: 'And if one member suffers, all the members suffer together; if a member is glorified, all the members rejoice together. For we are the body of Christ, and members in particular' (1 Cor. 12.26–27).

The Genesis text seems to suggest that the manifold that is humanity is in some way based on the distinction between the sexes. The Fathers, however, are not very good at handling what an American poet has called the 'archetypal cleft of sex'.[8] I am not sure we are much better, either. We (and they) can see that the relationship of man and woman forms the basis of the family and that that is the primary unit of human society. We can see (most of us; they, the Fathers, rarely) that the relationship is one that offers human beings the deepest human delight, but we (all!) recognize too that this 'archetypal cleft' lies behind the most painful and destructive aspects of human experience. Genesis, furthermore, seems to present the division into male and female as fundamental to what it is to be human, not just something that anticipates the conditions of the Fall, as many of the Fathers were tempted to think; and if fundamental to what it is to be human, fundamental to any kind of human society or community, including the Church. Even in the New Testament there are hints of this in the way in which the Church is spoken of as the (female) bride of the (male) Christ (see Eph. 5.25–32, and the Apocalypse of St John 21—22).

However, this verse from Genesis does suggest that we are not to consider human beings as individuals, but as bound together within the unity of humanity, a unity that is embodied in the communities to which we belong. The doctrine of the image of God embraces this aspect of what it is to be human, too, for if being in the image means that we have an affinity with God, that entails, too, that we have an affinity with one another, on the basis of which we find some kind of togetherness. And if the Church is the community embracing those who, in Christ, have set out on the path to the restoration of fallen humanity, then the community of the Church should give us some

---

[8] From 'Dodona: Asked of the Oracle', in *The Collected Poems of Amy Clampitt* (New York: Knopf, 1997), 207.

sense of what a true human community should be. Nevertheless, the Church is part of the fallen world, so we should not expect to find in any unambiguous way the ideal human community in the Church.

The New Testament gives us some pointers, and we can glean some others from the history of the Church. The apostle Paul has much to say about the nature of the community of the Church and its unity, though this very fact demonstrates how threatened this unity and harmony was in practice. To the Galatians, he affirms that 'in Christ Jesus you are all sons of God through faith . . . There is neither Jew nor Greek, there is neither slave nor free, there is neither male nor female; for you are all one in Christ Jesus' (Gal. 3.26, 28). National differences, rank and even the 'archetypal cleft' are to be transcended in the Church. And he talks of the way in which this is to be achieved: through the fruits of the Spirit, found in the Church, which are 'love, joy, peace, patience, kindness, goodness, faithfulness, gentleness, self-control' (Gal. 5.22–23). He speaks, too, of bearing 'one another's burdens' (Gal. 6.2), and of the 'more excellent way', that of love:

> Love is patient and kind, love is not jealous or boastful; it is not arrogant or rude. Love does not insist on its own way; it is not irritable or resentful; it does not rejoice at wrong, but rejoices in the right. Love bears all things, believes all things, hopes all things, endures all things.
>
> (1 Cor. 13.4–7)

The Church – one and many

What these suggestions as to the nature of Christian community add up to immediately is, I think, something like this. We are to think of the Church as many embraced by oneness, and oneness expressed in the many: both poles – the one and the many – are important, irreducible. It is in this sense, I think, that the doctrine of the Trinity is relevant to our understanding of Christian community, or communion. Not that the Trinity is some kind of model that we should try to emulate – that would be to think in too anthropomorphic terms, though such an idea has been very popular in the last few decades, not least among Orthodox – but rather that in the Trinity we see that neither one nor three are ultimate: at the very heart of reality, or the source of reality, there is both one and three, together.

So in human community, as it is meant to be, neither the one nor the many is ultimate; the many does not yield before the one, as if what mattered was the one community and the many has to be compressed into it (by some unitary authority, say), nor is the one simply to be thought of as some kind of harmony among the many, as if it were the individuals who were important and their harmony secondary. Another way of putting this is to say that we find our own identity as persons in the togetherness we share with others, and that unity is an expression of something that we genuinely hold in common.

Many ways of understanding human community either start with the individual or with the community, but it seems to me that what we are to learn in the Church is that neither the one nor the many is more fundamental: we find our identity through our communion with others, and yet we are not just units in a group, which is what really counts. When the apostle Paul talks about the human community that is the Church, he talks about ways of behaving that yield to the others and support the others, not ways of asserting ourselves over against the others. There is, to use a word we are familiar with in another context, a *kenosis*, a self-emptying, that enables us to make space for the others, and in that space allowed by the others to find ourselves.

In the history of the Church, the kind of community about which we learn most has always been a minority pursuit, though sometimes a large minority: monastic community. It is no wonder that the passage from Galatians referred to above (Gal. 5.22—6.2) is the passage from the Epistle (or 'Apostle', as it is called in the Orthodox rite) set for a monk or nun who lived in community. And yet, much monastic literature is marked by a sense of the fragility of human community in a fallen world: much stress is placed on obedience, as if the exercise of free will is most likely to be a misuse, and there is a good deal of fear about what came to be called 'particular friendships', again with fear of abuse driving out any attempt to consider what the place of true friendship might be.

Sobornost' and the Church

I want to take further this sense of the fundamental nature of community to what it is to be human by reflecting on a notion that has been made much of in Russian Orthodox theology since the middle of the nineteenth century, and that is the notion of *sobornost'*. The term is associated with the Slavophiles, especially Aleksei Khomiakov and Ivan Kireevsky, though it appears that the abstract noun *sobornost'* is not actually found in their writings.[9]

The word *sobornost'* is derived from the word used in the Slavonic version of the creed to translate *katholikos*, 'catholic'. It appears that some of the older texts of the Slavonic Creed simply transliterated *katholikos* as *katholichesky*, as did the Latin version and virtually all European versions, but in (or maybe by) the fifteenth century *katholichesky* was replaced by *soborny*.

It is often said that *soborny* is derived from the word for a council in Slavonic, *sobor*;[10] but I suspect the truth is more interesting. In replacing *katholichesky*, the Slavonic translators went back to the root meaning of *katholikos*, which is formed from the Greek *kath' holon*, 'according to the whole', and took the word to mean something like 'taken as a whole', 'gathered together'. So they used the word *soborny*, an adjective derived from the verb *sobrat'*, 'to gather together'. The word for council or synod, translating the Greek *synodos*, meaning a 'coming together', a 'gathering' and hence 'council', is *sobor*, so the use of *soborny* in the creed suggested that it is in a council that the Church manifests its nature.

In a remarkable way, then, the word *soborny* makes a link between the Church as catholic and the Church as conciliar: between the Church as proclaiming a truth that concerns everyone, and the Church as constituted by being gathered together by God. There is another word that seems to fit this vision of the Church: as well as *katholikos* and *synodos*, there is the word *synaxis*, another word for gathering together, which is one of the words used for the divine liturgy, the gathering together of the people of God in one place under the bishop. It is in this way – as gathering together into unity – that the Church can be seen to be an image of God, as St Maximos the Confessor suggests in his work of the divine liturgy, called *The Mystagogia*:

> For many and of nearly boundless number are the men, women and children who are distinct from one another and vastly different by birth and appearance, by race and language, by way of life and age, by opinions and skills, by manners and customs, by pursuits and studies, and still again by reputation, fortune, characteristics and habits: all are born into the Church and through it are reborn and recreated in the

---

[9] See *On Spiritual Unity: A Slavophile Reader* (trans. and ed. Boris Jakim and Robert Bird; Hudson, NY: Lindisfarne Books, 1998), 8, n. 1.

[10] *On Spiritual Unity*, 15.

Spirit. To all in equal measures it gives and bestows one divine form and designation: to be Christ's and to bear his name.[11]

The convergence of the Greek *synodos* and *katholikos* in the Slavonic *sobor/soborny* produces a happy association of ideas. The note of the Church, catholic or *soborny*, is manifest in its gathering together in unity humans of any kind, and this is manifest in the gathering together, the *synaxis*, in the church building (also in Russian *sobor*, from the Greek *katholikon*, for a public church, as opposed to a chapel) and in the councils, or synods, of the Church.

Sobornost', then, developed by the Slavophiles as an ecclesiological concept to account for what they regarded as the peculiarly Orthodox understanding of unity in the Church, is also, as it should be, a term to describe the fundamental nature of human community. As an ecclesiological concept, it suggests a vision of the Church as combining unity and freedom: the unity of the Orthodox Church is a free association of believers. Or, perhaps better, those who belong and within the Church find their true freedom, in opposition to what Khomiakov saw as the unity found in the Catholic Church, imposed by authority and encroaching on, or overriding, human freedom, and the so-called unity within the Protestant Churches, which is a free association of those who agree in their interpretation of the Scriptures and confessions – a unity purely human and thus inevitably quite fragile. As a term to describe the true nature of human community, it also draws together unity and freedom. Clearly some sort of distinction between human community and the community of the Church is needed, but ultimately it is artificial, for it is in Christ, in the Church, that human beings find their true humanity.

Khomiakov is often criticized for the vagueness of his notion of *sobornost'*, but that vagueness – or better, the lack of an exhaustive definition – seems to me intrinsic to the notion. For it is not some constitutional term that can be cashed in terms of legal norms; rather, it is an attempt to indicate the fundamental nature of human community, which springs from the religious nature of humanity, the realization that what is fundamental to being human is the capacity to respond to each other and to God, ultimately the capacity to open

---

[11] *Mystagogia* 1. 163–74 (ed. Christian Boudignon; CCSG, 69; Turnhout: Brepols, 2011); trans. modified: by G. C. Berthold, in *Maximus Confessor: Selected Writings* (London: SPCK, 1985), 187.

oneself in prayer. Khomiakov evokes this in a striking passage from his short pamphlet, *The Church Is One*:

> We know that those among us who fall, fall by themselves, but that no one is saved alone. Those who are saved are saved in the Church as her members and in unity with all her other members. When someone believes, that person is in a community of faith; when someone loves, that person is in a community of love; when someone prays, such a person is in a community of prayer. For this reason no one can rely on one's own prayers, and each in prayer asks the entire Church for intercession – not as though doubting the intercession of Christ, the one intercessor, but in confidence that the entire Church always prays for all her members. There pray for us all the angels, apostles, martyrs, patriarchs, and the most-high Mother of our Lord, and this holy union is the true life of the Church.[12]

We are saved in the Church, in unity with all her members.

It seems to me that Orthodox theology insists on the doctrine of deification, *theosis*, because recovering the fullness of the image will involve real changes in ourselves, changes that mean that the image of God in which we are created becomes more and more evident. We are to become transparent, as it were, to the image of God reflected in who we are most deeply. Others are to find in us, not the fragmented human beings that we are as a result of the Fall, but the love of God manifest in the image of God, for whose sake we have been created. In doing this we shall discover our true humanity: deification, as St Maximos makes so clear, is the restoration of our true humanity, not its diminishment or abandonment. And it is a change grounded in the amazing change that God himself embraced, when he became human for our sakes, not abandoning what he is – divinity – but assuming what he is not – humanity.

St Athanasios makes an affirmation that is repeated by one after another of the Fathers. 'The Word of God became human, that we might become god'.[13] This amazing exchange, founded in God's love, reveals that at the heart of what it is to be human is an openness to God and his love through which we are taken up into the divine life, and discover there what it is to be human, what God intended human life to be – communion with him in the Spirit.

---

[12] *On Spiritual Unity*, 48.
[13] *On the Incarnation*, 54.

7

Sacraments and icons: the place of matter in the divine economy

A chief captain of angels
Was sent from heaven
to say to the Mother of God, 'Hail!'
And as, at his bodiless voice,
Lord, he saw you embodied,
he was astounded and stood still . . .[1]

With these words the Akathist Hymn begins. It contains a play on words – a striking feature that runs through the whole of the Akathist Hymn – 'bodiless'–'embodied'. Plays on words in general throughout the Akathist – generally as here a contrast, or even contradiction – express primarily the paradox contained in the Incarnation – God become man – in particular the paradox of the virginal birth and conception, recalled at the end of every *ikos*: Hail, Bride unwedded! Here, with the first play on words, the contrast is between the bodilessness of the archangel and indeed the Lord, in his divine state, and the embodied nature of the Word Incarnate, initially as an embodied foetus in his mother's womb. The Incarnation is about the embodiment of God in human form, a human form he assumed from the blessed Virgin – one might almost say, the materialization of God.

Christian materialism

Some Orthodox theologians, such as Bulgakov, have spoken of a 'Christian materialism', and they are right: running through the history of the Church there has been a constant struggle against a tendency towards a false spiritualization, that opposes the spiritual to the material, and seeks flight from the material.

---

[1] *An Orthodox Prayer Book* (Eng. trans. Archimandrite Ephrem Lash; Milton under Wychwood: Fellowship of St Alban & St Sergius, 2009), 34.

This was an issue in the time of the New Testament: in the second epistle of John we read of those 'who will not acknowledge the coming of Jesus Christ in the flesh'. The apostle regards them as 'deceiver' and 'antichrist' (2 John 7), as we might expect from one who proclaimed that 'the Word became flesh' (John 1.14), and speaks of that 'which was from the beginning, which we have heard, which we have seen with our eyes, which we have looked upon and touched with our hands' (1 John 1.1). In the second century, in the context of what modern scholars call 'gnosticism', we encounter those called 'docetists', who thought that Jesus only 'appeared' (Greek: *dokeo*) to be human, but was not really. Many of the christological heresies, which we have already briefly looked at, have as part of their rationale a sense that God and the material were too set apart from each other to come together in the Incarnation: either it was not really God who was incarnate (Arianism, for example), or God and humanity had to be held apart in the Incarnation (Nestorianism, at least as the Orthodox regarded it). Again, in the iconoclast controversy, part of what inspired those who rejected icons was a sense that what God really requires of us is worship in spirit and in truth (cf. John 4.24), understood to mean something removed from the material.

In response to the iconoclasts, St John Damascene, the great champion of the making and veneration of icons, asserted:

> I do not venerate matter, I venerate the fashioner of matter, who became matter for my sake and accepted to dwell in matter and through matter worked my salvation, and I will not cease from reverencing matter, through which my salvation was worked . . .[2]

In his *Exposition of the Orthodox Faith*, John Damascene presents an understanding of the Christian faith that acknowledges fully that the human is twofold – both material and spiritual – so that the divine economy is not only concerned with the spiritual part, through teaching, for example, but just as much with the material part. His understanding of the place of matter is based fundamentally on the doctrine of creation: because matter is created out of nothing by God, there is nothing in it opposed to God, it is in itself good. And the enduring place of matter is evident in the Christian belief in

---

[2] *On Images* I. 16; translation in St John of Damascus, *Three Treatises on the Divine Images* (Crestwood, NY: St Vladimir's Seminary Press, 2003), 23.

the resurrection of the body from the dead, as opposed to any understanding of human destiny as being merely spiritual, or immaterial. This positive appreciation of matter is fundamental to the two aspects of Orthodox Christianity I want to consider now: icons and the sacraments.

Mystery or sacrament?

I have used the word 'sacrament', for that is the usual word in English to refer to baptism, the Eucharist, and so on. It is based on the Latin word *sacramentum*, which means a solemn oath (especially a military oath). The word used for these rites in Greek is quite different: *mysterion*, 'mystery' or 'secret' – derived from the root *mu-* and conveying a sense of something not to be uttered, to be kept silent (or even hidden). It is often said to be onomatopoeic: one compresses one's lips to pronounce the *m*. The word *mysterion* occurs once in the Gospels – when the Lord talks about the 'mystery of the kingdom of God [or heaven]', hidden to most, but revealed to the disciples (Matt. 13.11; Mark 4.11; Luke 8.10) – but quite frequently in the letters of the apostle Paul. It is usually transliterated in Latin versions of the New Testament by *mysterium*, but a few times it is translated by *sacramentum* (e.g., Eph. 5.32; 1 Tim. 3.16). Both are rather striking occasions – the first refers to marriage as a mystery signifying Christ and the Church, the second to the 'mystery of religion', Christ 'manifest in the flesh, justified in the Spirit, seen by angels, preached among the nations, believed in the world, received up in glory'.

It does, I think, make a difference what word we use. If we use the word sacrament then the link with the New Testament notion of mystery is concealed. If, however, we use the word mystery, *mysterion*, *tainstvo*, then we make evident their association with the mystery of Christ: 'the mystery hidden for ages and generations but now made manifest to his saints. To them God chose to make known how great among the Gentiles are the riches of the glory of this mystery, which is Christ in you, the hope of glory' (Col. 1.26–27). The mysteries are the ways in which the mystery of Christ is made manifest in the Church for the world.

The use of the word sacrament in the Latin West rather obscures the way in which the sacraments relate to the mystery of Christ.

98

Nevertheless, the word carries its own connotations, connotations derived not so much from its original use, or etymology, as from its Christian use to refer to something visible that manifests something hidden, or invisible. I think it will be useful to pursue the two paths opened up by both these words.

Mystery

First, mysteries: mysteries referring to or communicating the mystery of Christ. What is the mystery of Christ? It is the hidden purpose of God, his intention of uniting the whole of creation with himself: a purpose seemingly thwarted by human sin, but a purpose to which God remained faithful. The account of human history, and then the history of Israel, in the Old Testament bears witness to God's faithfulness. As we pray in the Liturgy of St Basil:

> For you did not utterly turn away from your creature, O Good One, nor forget the work of your hands, but you visited us in divers manners through your compassionate mercy. You sent Prophets, you performed deeds of power through your saints, who have been well-pleasing to you in every generation; you spoke to us through the mouth of your servants, the Prophets, announcing to us beforehand the salvation that was to come; you gave the law as a help; you appointed Angels as guardians.[3]

God's hidden purpose is fully revealed in the Incarnation of his Son, his death and resurrection: this is the mystery of Christ. It is a manifest mystery, a mystery that has been declared, a secret that has been exploded, as it were. And yet, at the same time, it remains a mystery, for we shall never fully understand what has been revealed and made manifest in Christ, for it is not a matter of information, but of participation in the restoration of all things in Christ: it entails deification, *theosis*.

The mysteries of the Church lead us to participate in the mystery of Christ, for the Church is the body of Christ: Christ is now manifest through the Church and its members. So when we think of the mysteries of the Church we are thinking of the ways in which Christ makes himself manifest in the world now. Christ is not limited to his Church; he can reveal himself in manifold ways through

---

[3] *The Divine Liturgy of our Father among the Saints Basil the Great* (trans. Archimandrite Ephrem; privately published; Manchester: St Andrew's Press, 2001), 29.

his creation – both through the created order itself, and also through men and women who with sincerity and love are open to the hidden mystery of Christ, the Word or *Logos* of God. But it is in the Church, in her mysteries, that we discover in its fullness the love of God, that heals and perfects and draws us into the unity of Christ.

Sacrament

The previous section described the path opened up by the term 'mystery'. What of the term 'sacrament'? In his letter to the apostle John, Dionysios remarks: 'Truly visible things are manifest images of things invisible' (*ep.* 10).[4] This seems to be presented as a general principle about the nature of reality: visible things point beyond themselves to the invisible; they have a meaning that cannot be confined to their visible, material reality.

In considering the idea that visible things have some significance that is not on the surface but needs teasing out, as it were, one often finds recourse to the notion of the symbol. In origin a symbol was a token that had been broken in two and the parts given to two people who in some way belonged to each other, or were committed to some venture; when the two parts were brought together again this common purpose and their commitment to it was reaffirmed. From this a symbol came to mean something that points beyond itself, something the meaning of which is not exhausted by what it seems to be. It encourages a way of looking at reality as possessing some hidden significance. Using things as symbols seems to be a very fundamental human practice: we are not content with things as they are, we confer on them, or find in them, meaning, a meaning that binds us together. The Anglo-Welsh poet and artist, David Jones, expressed very succinctly the nature of signs and symbols:

> A man can not only smell roses (some beasts may do that, for lavender is said to be appreciated in the Lion House) but he can and does and ought to pluck roses and he can predicate of roses such and such. He can make a *signum* of roses. He can make attar of roses. He can garland them and make anathemata of them. Which is, presumably, the *kind* of thing he is meant to do. Anyway, there's no one else can do it. Angels can't nor can the beasts. No wonder then that Theology regards the

---

[4] My translation. For a complete translation of Dionysios the Areopagite, see *Pseudo-Dionysius: The Complete Works* (trans. Colm Luibhéid; Mahwah, NJ: Paulist Press, 1987).

body as a unique good. Without body: without sacrament. Angels only: no sacrament. Beasts only: no sacrament. Man: sacrament at every turn and all levels of the 'profane' and 'sacred', in the trivial and in the profound, no escape from sacrament.[5]

Symbols are intimately bound up with the visible and the material; they invest the visible and material with a meaning that transcends them.

From very early on, Christians looked at the created order in just such a way. The first surviving account of the six days of creation – the *Hexaemeron* – by a Christian writer, Theophilos of Antioch, in a treatise defending Christianity in the second century presents the creation as full of hidden meaning: the sea, for instance, provides an image of the world or cosmos, for as the sea is not self-sufficient but depends on water from springs and rivers flowing into it to prevent it from becoming a parched, salty waste, so the cosmos needs the sweetness and compassion of God if it is not to sink into a state of sin and evil.[6] The luminaries of the fourth day contain 'a pattern and type of a great mystery': the sun is a type of God in its permanence, whereas the moon with its constant waxing and waning is a type of the human, in his vacillating state, and the moon's regular rebirth is a sign of the future resurrection.[7] Theophilos finds God's 'manifold wisdom' in the animal world which reflects, as in a mirror, many traits that appear in humanity. Theophilos does not go into much detail – he is addressing pagans and simply concerned to show how Christianity, far from being a strange wisdom, is rooted in the created order – but later Christians develop further Theophilos' intuition of a visible creation, full of hidden mysteries.

Images and symbols

This sense of the created order as consisting of 'forests of symbols', rather to misuse a phrase of Baudelaire's, suggests a way of looking at the world as in some sense 'sacramental'. The ideas of mystery and sacrament converge, and at the point of convergence we find the human. As David Jones notes, it is something peculiar to human kind

---

[5] David Jones, *Epoch and Artist* (London: Faber & Faber, 1959), 166–7, from an essay, 'Art and Sacrament' (143–79).

[6] *Ad Autolycum* 14; translation from Theophilus of Antioch, *Ad Autolycum* (ed. and trans. Robert M. Grant; Oxford: Oxford University Press, 1970).

[7] Theophilos, *Ad Autolycum* 15.

to take the material world and treat it symbolically, and that relates to the point already noted in St John Damascene that the human is essentially twofold: spiritual and material, soul and body.

That duality makes of the human a creature existing on the borderland, belonging to two different worlds that are brought together in his existence. And it is, we realize, the mystery of Christ that lies behind that duality: the duality of the human reflecting the profound duality in Christ, perfect God and perfect man. The mystery of Christ in the Incarnation is intended to bring to perfection in man his role as a being who relates, who brings together – something that culminates in human kind's bridging even the divide between the uncreated and the created in his deification. That was always the purpose of the mystery of Christ, but in the circumstances brought about by the Fall, that purpose is now to restore to human kind the cosmic role of bond of the cosmos that he was meant to exercise through being in the image of God: something we explored in the last chapter.

Here, a further term is introduced – the image, the *eikon*, the icon – which is closely related to the notion of the symbol. In his *Exposition of the Orthodox Faith*, John Damascene begins his presentation of the theology of the icon by affirming that in the beginning God made human kind in his own image.[8] In making images, human beings are only imitating God: that is John's contention. Human beings are not simply in the image of God, as we have already discussed; they make images, and make images as a way of understanding and communicating. For the Damascene, images are not just illustrations, good, bad or indifferent, they are essential if we are to understand anything at all.

Twice in his treatises in defence of icons, John gives lists of the different kinds of images, or icons. The first is the natural image – as the Son is an image of God the Father, so that he can say, 'He who has seen me has seen the Father' (John 14.9); second, there is the kind of image that exists in the mind of God of what God is going to bring about through his providence; third, there is the human, created in God's image; fourth, there are material images and symbols used in Scripture to help us glimpse something of the nature of God and the angelic realm; fifth, there are images in the Old Testament that

---

[8] John Damascene, *Exposition of the Orthodox Faith* 89.

prefigure the fulfilment in the New – the burning bush, prefiguring the Ever-Virgin Mary, is an example John gives; finally, there are images, whether written or depicted, that recall events and persons of the past.[9] It seems to me that what John is doing in sketching out this list is showing how it is through images that we understand anything – from the mysteries of the Godhead to our understanding of human existence in history.

What all this adds up to, I think, is that openness to recognizing images and symbols in reality is necessary, if we are to unlock the mysteries of existence and, in particular, to understand the nature of the cosmos created by God and brought to its final purpose through the mystery of Christ in his Incarnation, death and resurrection. Particular sacraments, or mysteries, fit into that broad pattern written into the nature of reality by the divine will in creation.

Seven sacraments?

Conventionally, we speak of seven sacraments – baptism, chrism or *myron*, the Eucharist, the sacrament of confession (repentance and forgiveness), the sacrament of anointing (for healing of soul and body), marriage and ordination. But this list of seven really reflects the concerns of twelfth-century scholasticism in the Western Middle Ages, which sought to define narrowly the sacraments by reference to institution by Christ himself, doubtless seduced too by the mystique of the number seven, and distinguish them from other sacred acts, which were designated sacramentals, not sacraments proper.

The notion of the seven sacraments was presented to the Eastern Church as part of the faith that they would be required to accept in return for union with the Western Church (and military support against the encroaching threat of Muslim Turks), first of all at the union Council of Lyon in 1274. Later on, in the context of trying to relate Eastern Orthodox theology to post-Reformation theology, both Catholic and Protestant, Orthodox theologians came to think in terms of seven sacraments, because, in contrast to the Protestants, they did have all the rites the Catholics regarded as sacraments. The notion of seven sacraments came to be incorporated into Orthodox Catechisms; for example, the Catechism issued by Metropolitan

---

[9] *On Images* III. 18–23; cf. I. 9–13.

Philaret of Moscow, where it expands the section on the tenth article of the creed, on baptism.[10]

Many Orthodox theologians nowadays, without suggesting that any of the 'seven' should be abandoned, regard the limitation of the sacraments, or mysteries, to seven as an aspect of Western medieval theology that fits ill with the approach of Orthodox theology, and I would count myself among that number. However, the traditional seven sacraments (though the tradition is, I repeat, not very firmly rooted in the Orthodox tradition) relate conveniently to the structures of the Church and the rhythms of human life. I shall therefore start with them, and then go on to talk about other sacraments, and finally about icons – all of which I understand as manifestations of the mystery of Christ revealed in a sacramental universe.

Even the seven sacraments seem to me not a list of individual sacraments, equal to one another, rather they seem to consist of groups. There are two fundamental sacraments: holy baptism and the Eucharist or the divine liturgy. Baptism itself embraces a group of sacraments: for the rite of initiation in the Orthodox Church includes anointing with *myron*, or chrismation, which is not really a separate sacrament in the rite of initiation; rather, the rite of initiation consists of a number of sacramental actions. Fundamental among these are baptism, that is, being dipped into water, anointing with *myron*, and receiving the holy gifts of the body and blood of Christ, but they include a pre-baptismal anointing with olive oil, clothing in a white garment, the giving of a baptismal cross, which Orthodox Christians wear from that day onwards, generally under their clothes, the giving of a lighted candle, and also the offering of the hair of the head: tonsuring.

It seems to me unhelpful to think of three sacraments and several lesser sacramental acts; it makes much more sense to think of a single act of initiation, comprising several symbolic or sacramental acts. Some of these symbolic acts have a life of their own, outside the rite of initiation: most important, Holy Communion, for while this is the conclusion of the rite of initiation, it is also the beginning of regular participation in the body and blood of Christ in the Eucharist, which will continue throughout the life of the new Christian.

---

[10] Metropolitan Philaret of Moscow, *Catechism of the Orthodox Church* (repr., Willits, CA, n.d.), 53–65.

The anointings – with oil and with *myron* – also have roles outside the rite of initiation. Anointing with blessed olive oil is the central action of the sacrament of healing, the *evchelaion* or *soborovanie* (the Greek term meaning something like 'blessing of oil', as the alternative Slavonic term *eleosvyashchenie* suggests; the other Slavonic term refers to the *sobor*, or assembly of [seven] priests, envisaged by the full rite).[11] Anointing with *myron* or chrism has at least two other uses: in the consecration of churches, which are anointed with chrism, and in the solemn reception into the Orthodox Church of Christians baptized outside it. Reception into the Orthodox Church is moreover an act of individual reconciliation with the Church, which points to a parallel with the sacrament of confession, or repentance (penance), in which the penitent is restored to, or assured of, full communion with the Church. This is generally administered simply by a prayer of forgiveness and absolution, but it can be seen as an extension of 'baptism for the forgiveness of sins' – a reawakening to the grace of forgiveness already given in baptism. Already one can see another reason for Orthodox dissatisfaction with a tidy list of seven sacraments, for there are interrelationships between the different sacraments; they are not freestanding acts or rites.

The sacramental structure of the Church

Within the sacraments already mentioned, one can discern two – not altogether separate – strands. One strand has to do with the structure of the Church: baptism, the rite of initiation and the divine liturgy, the gathering together of the people of God as the Church. To this strand could be added one of the 'seven' sacraments, the sacrament of ordination to the ranks of deacon, priest and bishop, as well as the lesser rites of admission as a reader or subdeacon. For the structure of the Church does not simply emerge from within the community of the Church; the bishop, though elected, is not simply an elected leader, deriving his authority from the Church community. Rather the bishop represents Christ's ministry to the Church, not simply in the Church; he represents the apostolate, the sending into the world for the sake of the world, 'for the life of the world'.

---

[11] Chrism is a mixture of olive oil and a highly aromatic substance based on balsam, to which are added various herbs and spices, prepared according to a complex recipe during Lent, and blessed in Holy Week by Patriarchs only in the Eastern tradition.

Another 'structural' sacrament, not included in the 'seven', but often treated sacramentally, is monastic consecration: the tonsuring and wearing of the *rason*, the giving of the little and the great schema – these are not just symbols of rank within the monastic order (indeed they are hardly that at all), but signs of a life of prayer, consecrated to God in community or in solitude. The life of the Church depends on the prayer of all who belong to it, but especially on the prayer of those who dedicate their lives to God in a more whole-hearted way than is possible for those who live in the world – as well as the prayers of those who have gone before us, the saints and the martyrs, and above all, the Virgin Mother of God.

The sacramental shape of human life

The other strand is concerned with the progress and rhythms of human life: baptism as the beginning of one's life as a Christian, generally for many nowadays correlative with birth (though in the post-Constantinian world we are entering, that correlation is becoming less uniform); Holy Communion as our 'daily bread', our food for the journey to eternal life; confession and absolution as our way of being restored to the path from which we have strayed; the sacrament of anointing, for healing of soul and body.

The sacrament of marriage belongs here, too, though it also has a 'structural' role, for marriage is the basis of the family, the fundamental unit in human society, whether civil society or that of the Church. Whatever else may be provided to nurture children, the nurture children receive from their parents – to enable them both for the natural communities of village/town and nation and for the supernatural community of the Church – remains fundamental. But marriage is also commitment to life together with another, to the asceticism implicit in trying to give someone else a part in one's life, as well as the comfort that the presence of another can provide. In this sense, marriage (in this way, parallel to monastic consecration) offers one kind of route through life, and therefore belongs to the 'progress and rhythms of human life'. The Orthodox Church (maybe not for entirely transparent reasons) recognizes both the beauty of married love and its fragility; if the ideal is, as the Lord made clear, a union for life, the reality often falls short of this, and the Orthodox Church has proved willing to accept 'the admission of inconsistencies inherent in life itself, and of the impossibility of overcoming them by the imposition of a uniformity greater than life will bear'.[12]

To this strand concerned with the Christian life, one could well add the funeral service. Dionysios the Areopagite, in his *Ecclesiastical Hierarchy*, includes it along with ordination and monastic consecration as one of the ceremonies that he discusses in the second rank, after the first rank of 'rites' or *teletai* consisting of baptism (or Illumination, as he calls it), the Eucharist (or the Synaxis, or 'gathering together') and the Sacrament of Myron. This is perhaps why the funeral service is sometimes included among the mysteries (which is the word Dionysios uses: the 'mystery of the holy departed').[13] The solemn farewell, the last kiss, the beginning of the days of prayer for the departed: all these comprise a 'mystery of holy death'.

Sacramental symbolism

The prayers for the sacraments, or mysteries, are full of a symbolism that relates what is happening to the particular person to a much larger, all-encompassing world or cosmos. Let me give two examples, the first from the service of baptism. The actual baptism – or dipping, which is what the Greek means – is preceded by the blessing of the water, and there being mingled with it olive oil. The prayer for the blessing of the water runs thus:

> Great are you, O Lord, and wonderful are your works; and no word will be adequate to sing the praise of your wonders. For as by your will you brought the universe from non-existence into being, by your might you uphold creation and by your providence you direct the world. From four elements you composed the world, with four seasons you crowned the circle of the year. All the spiritual Powers tremble before you. The sun sings your praise, the moon glorifies you, the stars entreat you, the light obeys you, the deeps tremble before you, the springs are your servants. You stretched out the heaven like a curtain; you established the earth on the waters; you walled in the sea with sand; you poured out the air for breathing. Angelic Powers minister to you, the choirs of Archangels worship you, the many-eyed Cherubim and the six-winged seraphim, as they stand and fly around you, veil themselves in fear of your unapproachable glory. For you,

---

[12] Words of the poet and Anglican churchman, T. S. Eliot, in another context: see Eliot, *Selected Essays* (London: Faber & Faber, 1963), 376.

[13] Title of the second part of *Ecclesiastical Hierarchy* 7.

God uncircumscribed, without beginning and ineffable, came upon earth taking the form of a slave, being found in the likeness of mortals. For through the compassion of your mercy, Master, you could not endure to watch the human race being tyrannized by the devil, but you came and saved us. We confess your grace, we proclaim your mercy, we do not conceal your benevolence. You set at liberty the generations of our nature, you sanctified a virgin womb by your birth. All creation sang your praise when you appeared. For you, our God, were seen on earth and lived among mortals. You also sanctified the streams of Jordan by sending down to them from heaven your all-holy Spirit, and you crushed the heads of the dragons that lurked there. Therefore, O King, lover of mankind, be present now too, through the visitation of your Holy Spirit, and sanctify this water. Give it the grace of redemption, the blessing of Jordan. Make it a source of incorruption, a gift of sanctification, a deliverance from sins, a destruction of demons. Make it unapproachable by hostile powers and filled with angelic strength . . . Master of all things, declare this water to be water of redemption, water of sanctification, cleansing of flesh and spirit, untying of bonds, forgiveness of offences, enlightenment of soul, washing of rebirth, renewal of spirit, gift of adoption, garment of incorruption, source of life . . . Manifest yourself, Lord, in this water, and grant that the one being baptized in it may be transformed for the putting off of the old self that is corrupted after the desires of deception, and may put on the new that is renewed after the image of the One who created him/her. So that, planted in the likeness of your death through baptism, he/she may also become a partaker in your resurrection, and having guarded the gift of the Holy Spirit and increased the deposit of grace, may receive the prize of his/her high calling and be numbered with the firstborn, whose names are inscribed in heaven, in you our God and Lord, Jesus Christ . . .

This long and beautiful prayer moves from water as one of the four cosmic elements, through the historical waters of Jordan in which the Lord was baptized, to the water now being blessed for baptism. The one to be baptized is participating in the renewal of Creation, not just taking a step towards his or her personal salvation.

The same cosmic dimension is manifest in the prayer for the blessing of olive oil:

Master, Lord God of our fathers, who sent out a dove to those in Noah's ark, with a branch of olive in its beak as sign of reconciliation and salvation from the flood, and through these things prefigured the mystery of grace; who have given the fruit of the olive for the completion of your holy Mysteries; who through it both filled those under the Law with the Holy Spirit, and made perfect those under grace; do you yourself bless this olive oil also by the power, operation and descent of your Holy Spirit, so that it may become an anointing of incorruption, a weapon of righteousness, renewal of soul and body, a driving away of every operation of the devil, for the removal of all evils from those who are anointed with it in faith, or who partake of it to your glory and that of your Only-Begotten Son and your all-holy, good, and life-giving Spirit, now and for ever, and to the ages of ages.[14]

The other example I want to take is from the ceremonies that surround the receiving of Holy Communion. The holy gifts are given to the laity on a spoon, called in Greek *lavis* – a word which does not really mean a spoon, but rather a pair of tongs. The reference is to the vision of Isaias in Isaias 6, when the prophet saw the Lord seated on a throne, high and raised up, the whole house being full of his glory. Around him were standing the seraphim, crying, 'Holy, holy, holy is the Lord Sabaoth, the whole earth is full of his glory!' Isaias is filled with a sense of sin and unworthiness. One of the seraphim takes a burning coal from the altar with a pair of tongs, a *lavis*, and touches the prophet's lips with it, saying, 'Behold, this has touched your lips, your iniquity is taken away and your sin purged'.

The use of the word *lavis* for the spoon recalls the vision of the prophet, which has already been evoked in the *Sanctus* in the eucharistic prayer, when we join with the heavenly hosts, 'singing, crying, shouting the triumphal hymn, and saying: Holy, holy, holy, Lord of hosts; heaven and earth are full of your glory. Hosanna in the highest. Blessed is he who comes in the name of the Lord. Hosanna in the highest.' The experience of Isaias is recalled again in the words the priest uses after giving Holy Communion – 'Behold, this has touched your lips, your iniquity is taken away and your sin purged' – the very words of the seraphim. The communicant is not simply receiving communion for him- or herself, but standing with the hosts of heaven, with the prophet, with the saints and the Mother of God, with all the people of God who have received communion over the centuries.[15]

---

[14] Translations taken from the website <http://www.anastasis.org.uk/baptism.htm>, accessed 9.4.2012 (the translations are by Archimandrite Ephrem [Lash]).

[15] For the texts referred to, see *The Divine Liturgy of our Father among the Saints John Chrysostom* (Oxford: Oxford University Press, 1995), 31–2 (for the *Sanctus*), 44–6 (for the rite of Communion).

Symbolism and sacramental transformation

There is one point I have not touched on, which I may be accused of obscuring by laying such stress on the symbolic character of the mysteries or sacraments. For the sacraments are not merely symbols, one might say; the elements – water, bread and wine, oil – have been changed, transformed, they are no longer ordinary water, bread, wine and oil. That is true, but there is a danger, and certainly there has been in the past, of concentrating too much on the change, and ignoring the wealth of symbols that have come to accompany the sacramental rites, as if the only thing that matters is the ontological change in the bread and wine, for example, while the rest of the symbolic structure could be dispensed with (and has been in ceremonies such as a 'low mass', which simply concentrates on the 'essentials').

It seems to me to be dangerous to think of the 'merely symbolic', for the use of symbols alters the way we look at things, the way we relate to people – it does effect a change, which can be very profound. Nonetheless, the language of change is very important in Orthodox understanding of the sacraments. At the time of the iconoclast controversy in the eighth and ninth centuries, the question of the eucharistic change was clarified by the Orthodox affirming that the Eucharist cannot be regarded, as the Iconoclasts did, as simply an icon, or type, of Christ: in the Eucharist the bread and wine are changed into Christ himself, for Christ is really present in the Eucharist – really and permanently present, as the Liturgy of the presanctified gifts makes clear. There is a real change in the water blessed for baptism and the oil blessed for healing – they accomplish something that would not be achieved by ordinary water and ordinary oil, though they remain visibly the same as ordinary water and oil. And in the case of the Eucharist, the bread and wine offered and consecrated are changed into the holy body and precious blood of Christ.

But the change needs to be put in a broader context, if we are to grasp its significance. If the notion of the change is isolated, there is the danger of trying to find some change analogous to the kind of change that takes place, for example, in a chemical reaction – precisely what the Latin doctrine of transubstantiation was seeking to avoid, in insisting that the change only takes place at the level of being, and not at any perceptible level, whether appearance or anything else that could be detected by human methods of assessment.

As the Reformation debates made clear, that danger was not always avoided either by those who insisted on the eucharistic change, or by those who denied it.

The wider context is made clear if we look at the prayer of invocation, or *epiklesis*, in the anaphora, or eucharistic prayer, of St John Chrysostom, the one most commonly used in the Orthodox Church. There the priest prays:

> Also we offer you this spiritual worship without shedding of blood, and we ask, pray and implore you: send down your Holy Spirit upon us and upon these gifts here set forth, and make this bread the precious body of your Christ, and what is in this cup the precious blood of your Christ, changing them by your Holy Spirit.

The invocation to the Holy Spirit is for him to descend on 'us' and the 'gifts'. We pray that the Holy Spirit may change the gifts of bread and wine into the precious body and blood of Christ, and that the Holy Spirit, coming on us, may work a change in us who receive them,

> so that those who partake of them may obtain vigilance of soul, forgiveness of sins, communion of your Holy Spirit, fulness of your kingdom, freedom to speak in your presence, not judgment or condemnation.[16]

For the wider context of change is the change that Christ came to effect through his Incarnation – in which God paradoxically accepted change, remaining what he was, God, and assuming what he was not, humanity: the change of all human kind into the image and likeness of God in which and for which we were created. This is one of the fundamental reasons why we Orthodox talk about deification; for what is offered to us by the Incarnate Christ, through the Eucharist and through our being faithful in our discipleship, is a change that will reach to the roots of our being – not some change simply in how we are regarded, nor even a change in our behaviour (though that will certainly take place), but a fundamental change so that the roots from which our actions flow are transformed, deified, and what others experience at our hands is the cherishing love of God himself.

The language of symbolism does not conflict with the language of change in the sacraments, for what the symbols themselves point to

---

[16] *Liturgy of St John Chrysostom*, 33–4.

is the change involved in the whole cosmos, through the human and with the human, as it is drawn more and more deeply into union with God. If, as I have suggested, we emphasize the symbolic world within which the sacraments or mysteries operate, then we shall see the world of the sacraments opening up, and indeed corresponding more closely to the way the notion of sacrament or mystery is used by the Fathers.

We have already seen an expansion in what counts as a sacrament or mystery, by including monastic consecration and the funeral rites. Many other things are treated as sacramental by the Fathers: the Lord's Prayer, for instance, or – a little more obviously – the sign of the cross.[17] The action of the sign of the cross is very ancient (our first evidence takes us back to the second century), and in current Orthodox practice it accompanies every action of our life – getting up, going to bed, before meals, before any significant task, before setting out on a journey . . . The idea of the cosmic cross – reaching from heaven to earth, and drawing together in its embrace things set furthest apart – is a powerful symbol, giving concrete form to the apostle Paul's prayer in Ephesians:

> that according to the riches of his glory he may grant you to be strength-ened with might through his Spirit in the inner man, and that Christ may dwell in your hearts through faith; and you, being rooted and grounded in love, may have power to comprehend with all the saints what is the breadth and length and height and depth, and to know the love of Christ which surpasses knowledge, that you may be filled with all the fullness of God.   (Eph. 3.16–19)

This same idea finds more elaborate expression in Saint Irenaeus:

> And since He is the Word of God who invisibly pervades the whole creation, and encompasses its length, breadth, height and depth – for by the Word of God everything is administered – so too was the Son of God crucified in these fourfold dimensions, having been imprinted in the form of the cross in everything; for it was necessary for him, becoming visible, to make manifest his form of the cross in everything, that He might demonstrate, by His visible form on the cross, His activ-ity which is on the invisible level, for it is He who illumines the 'heights',

---

[17] On the sign of the cross in Orthodox practice and theology, see Andreas Andreopoulos, *The Sign of the Cross: The Gesture, the Mystery, the History* (Brewster, MA: Paraclete Press, 2006).

that is, the things in heaven, and holds the 'deeps', which is beneath the earth, and stretches the 'length' from the East to the West, and who navigates the 'breadth' of the northern and southern regions, inviting the dispersed from all sides to the knowledge of the Father.[18]

Icons

From the perspective we have reached, icons can be seen as a particular extension of the symbolic world, founded on matter, that we have been exploring in this chapter. Icons, images – of Christ, the Mother of God and the saints – came to be used widely in Christianity, not just as pictures on panels or walls (frescoes), but on sacred vessels, garments, banners and even more intimate objects such as boxes and rings. They are objects of devotion, rather than works of art (though many of them are works of art of superlative quality); they are there to accompany our prayer, to mediate to us the presence of those to whom we pray; they are not there for aesthetic contemplation (though many of them are worthy of that). Unlike symbols, they work more directly through likeness; it is through likeness that they recall the people whom they depict, though the concept of likeness appropriate to icons has evolved to fulfil the purpose of mediating a prayerful presence, rather than a photographic likeness. Their justification is manifold – and unlike other aspects of Christian worship and practice explicit, as a result of the century-long iconoclast controversy from the eighth to the ninth century in the Byzantine Empire.

There is the justification I have already referred to, asserted most clearly by St John Damascene, that images or icons are fundamental to the kind of understanding available to human beings who are twofold in nature, both bodily and spiritual. Both icons and sacraments make sense only to beings with this twofold nature, for they are concerned with holding together the two realms that converge in the human. The most fundamental justification, however, is the Incarnation itself: if God appeared in a human form, then it must be possible to depict him in a human form.

A corollary of that is what I have already referred to as 'Christian materialism': matter is God's creation; it is not to be despised; it is

---

[18] Irenaeus, *Demonstration* 34; in St Irenaeus of Lyons, *On the Apostolic Preaching* (trans. and ed. John Behr; Crestwood, NY: St Vladimir's Seminary Press, 1997), 62. Cf. Athanasius, *On the Incarnation* 16.

precious; it is capable of disclosing to us the creative power of the God who created it. It is only because we are material beings that we can participate in God in the Eucharist, a privilege denied to purely spiritual beings such as angels. On that basis, John Damascene even argued that we could be regarded as higher beings than the angels, since we are capable of participating in God more richly than they are.[19]

This Christian materialism has implications, that we have already broached, for our attitude to the natural world: there is something sacred about matter, it is not 'material' for our disposal. A sacramental vision of the universe, a sense of the world as full of mysteries, is one that can contribute powerfully to the challenges posed us by the power we have in our hands as a result of the development of technology.

The importance of John Damascene's emphasis on the image becomes clear when we consider the alternatives: either a conceptual theology that is concerned with rational constructs – God as the central part of some philosophical understanding of the universe – or an agnosticism in which we lose any confidence in understanding at all. In contrast, a theology based on images can recognize the fundamental mystery that enshrouds the Godhead, the mystery that God is; it can embrace a fundamental apophaticism, and yet have some way of gesturing towards this ultimate mystery. It is as if the recognition of the place of images enables us to recognize, too, the fundamental place of apophaticism – denial of concepts – in our understanding of God, for images are playful and partial; they engage us, they do not give us ideas over which we have some kind of rational control. The great living Greek philosopher and theologian, Christos Yannaras, once put it like this: 'The apophatic attitude leads Christian theology to use the language of poetry and images for the interpretation of dogmas much more than the language of conventional logic and schematic concepts'.[20]

The image or icon is part of a whole approach to theology, an approach that sees theology as illuminating the journey of the Christian into God, rather than some speculative enterprise. I want to draw this out by dwelling a little on various general points about icons and then going on to discuss some particular icons.

---

[19] See John Damascene, *On Images* III. 26; *On the Two Wills of Christ* 16, 30 (translation of the former, with footnote, St John of Damascus, *Three Treatises on the Divine Images*, 103–4).
[20] Christos Yannaras, *Elements of Faith: An Introduction to Orthodox Theology* (Edinburgh: T. & T. Clark, 1991), 71.

Icons and the 'in-between'

My first point concerns the way in which icons occupy a kind of 'in-between space', the way in which the icon is essentially something *between* – between God and human kind, between heaven and earth, between the realm of the saints and the realm of human affairs.

This sense of 'in-betweenness' can be negotiated in various ways. The intellectual discipline of theology is concerned with forging, or at least understanding, a relationship between God and man, God and the universe. Politics and political figures can function in this way, too: the earthly state can be understood as reflecting some eternal reality. Understandings of how reality is peopled can be concerned with the 'in-between': beings such as angels, or demons, can be thought of as mediating between an upper world and a lower world. Prayer and mysticism is a further way of exploring the relationship 'in between'. But the icon is a visual and immediate way of designating the in-between: the surface of the icon lies along this in-between. We stand on one side, and on the other side are the figures or events depicted in the icons.

Various artistic techniques were developed to bring out the significance of the icon as in-between. The use of perspective in icons does not separate us from what is depicted, as does the use of linear perspective that became normal in the West from the Renaissance onwards; rather, the use of perspective is intended to create a space that embraces both what is depicted in the icon and the one who beholds the icon. The beholder of the icon, as it were, finds him- or herself passing through the in-between and entering this other world. St Stephen the Younger, one of the martyrs to the cause of the icons under the iconoclast emperor, Constantine V, affirmed that 'the icon is said to be a door that opens the mind created in accordance with God to the inward likeness of the model'.[21]

Celtic spirituality, both Christian and pagan, sometimes speaks of places where the boundary between heaven and earth becomes 'thin': as if at such places you could almost touch the heavenly realm. The icon represents such 'thinness'. I would like to speculate that it was a sense of such thinness that led to the tradition of icons being flat:

---

[21] *Life of St Stephen the Younger* 26 (in: *La Vie d'Étienne le Jeune par Étienne le Diacre* [ed. Marie-France Auzépy; Aldershot: Valorium, 1996], 122).

three-dimensional figures, even three-dimensional relief (though to a much lesser extent) makes of them too much objects in themselves, interposed between the spiritual world and this world, rather than simply marking out a boundary that they enable us to pass.

This notion of 'in-betweenness' affects the form of holiness attributed to the icon. Some of the defenders of the icons made the point that the holiness of the icon was not something added to it – by a priestly blessing, say – but something intrinsic in its being an image or icon. It was because it was an image of the reality depicted that it provided access to that reality, and in providing access to that reality came to partake of the holiness of the people or events depicted. If we behold the icon of the resurrection – in Orthodox use, the icon of Christ rescuing from Hades the whole of human kind, beginning with the forebears, Adam and Eve – we see the power of the risen Christ over death, and are able to make contact with that power, as it were. It is a power that reaches us. Or an icon of the Mother of God, introducing us to her son: the face of the one 'full of grace' draws us to Christ.

The icon and the face

This leads me on to another point associated with the icon: the centrality of the face. When we look at icons, it is the faces of those depicted that we are drawn to, a face or faces, turned towards us, modestly, not glaringly. As we gaze at the icon we enter into something of a face-to-face relationship. The only faces depicted on icons in profile are those of people to whom we are not to relate – Judas, for instance, in the icon of the Mystical Supper.

The face, or countenance, plays an important role in the Scriptures. We are to seek after the face of God (Ps. 23.6), we beg that God will not 'turn away his face from us' (Ps. 21.24), and at the same time ask that God will 'turn away [his] face from our sins' (Ps. 50.9). God's face represents his regard for us: we want to live in the light of his countenance, and yet fear that his gaze will search out our sins and bring punishment. More deeply there is a tradition that says that one cannot see God's face and live: something usually affirmed in the context of an exception. Jacob says after wrestling with the Lord: 'I have seen God face to face and my life has been preserved!' (Gen. 32.30), and when Moses asks to see God's glory, he is told that

116

no one 'can see God's face and live'. Yet Moses is granted a vision of God's glory, from behind, as it were. And yet again elsewhere God says that he spoke with Moses 'mouth to mouth' (Num. 12.8). The apostle Paul, too, speaks of seeing God 'face to face', in contrast with what we know now – seeing God in puzzling reflections in a mirror, *per speculum in aenigmate.*

It is through the faces in the icon that we are drawn into a relationship with the saints, Christ and the Mother of God. The face of Christ is the very face of God himself, and the saints are those who have seen the face of God. The Virgin Mother of God bears the face of the mother that gazed on her child, the Son of God: that face-to-face relationship in which the Incarnate Christ himself came to experience the nature of human relationship.

Moreover, the face is another example of the in-between; the face is physical, material, but it speaks to us of the soul of the one whose face we behold. The Russian philosopher, Nikolai Berdyaev, remarks: 'The vision of another person's countenance, the expression of his eyes, can often be a spiritual revelation. The eyes, the gestures, the words – all these are infinitely more eloquent of a man's soul than of his body.'[22] The very terminology (at least among the Slavs) used to describe the surface of the icon draws attention to the significance of the face, for the area bearing the face on the icon is called *lichnoe* (from the Russian *litso*, a face), and is treated differently from the rest of the icon, called *dolichnoe*, in the painting of the icon.

Being in between, 'thinness', being imbued, in some way, with holiness, drawing us into a face-to-face encounter: all this is effected by the icon. Icons, then, fulfil a variety of functions. First of all, they remind us that the boundary between heaven and earth is indeed thin. The apostle John reminds us: 'Greater is he that is in you, than he that is in the world' (1 John 4.4). Christians find in icons confirmation of this truth: icons bear witness to the reality of the communion of the saints, of those who have shared in Christ's triumph over death, of those who know a life that transcends death. And in witnessing to the communion of saints, they remind us that we belong to that communion, that the saints care for us, that we can turn to them – as we might turn to our friends and relatives – for support and prayer.

---

[22] Nicolas Berdyaev, *Solitude and Society* (trans. George Reavey; London: Greenwood Press, 1938), 109.

Icons and the Mother of God

Without doubt, the most popular of the saints is the Virgin Mary, the Mother of God: the one who gave God her humanity, so that he could become human, become one of us. Mary, then, incorporates everything that the icon incorporates: she became the place where God came to dwell. For nine months, as she bore Christ, the Godman, she was the place where God was dwelling among human kind. She became, quite literally, a living Temple, and remains the one who made God present in human form. She offers us her son as the God we are to worship; when she turns to God in prayer, she is turning to the one who is her son.

It is striking how, right from the beginning, in the second-century *Protevangelium of James*, reflection on Mary relates her to the Temple. In the *Protevangelium*, this is done in narrative form: Mary is brought up in the Temple; at the moment of the annunciation she is spinning the red and purple thread for the veil of the Temple, that will be rent in two at the moment of the crucifixion – as recorded in the Gospels. The Jewish Temple itself, and many of the objects found therein – the ark of the covenant, the rod of Aaron that burst into blossom, the jar containing the ointment – are seen as prefiguring the Virgin Mother of God: the Temple and the ark of the covenant, and the jar with the ointment, contain God as she contained in her womb the divine foetus; the rod that blossomed miraculously symbolizes the virginal conception and birth – the belief that Mary conceived and gave birth while still remaining a virgin.

What we see in narrative form in the *Protevangelium of James* takes on more lyrical form in the later hymns and songs to the Mother of God. The most famous of these songs is the so-called Akathist Hymn – *akathistos* being Greek for not standing, the hymn being generally sung in procession. One section of the Akathist goes thus:

> We sing your offspring
> and all raise to you our hymn
> as a living temple, Mother of God.
> For having dwelt in your womb,
> the Lord who holds all things in his hand
> sanctified, glorified you, and taught
> all to cry out to you:
> Hail, tabernacle of God the Word,

Hail, greater Holy of Holies.
Hail, Ark gilded by the Spirit,
Hail, inexhaustible treasure of life.
Hail, precious diadem of Orthodox kings,
Hail, honoured boast of devout priests.
Hail, unshakeable tower of the Church,
Hail, unbreachable wall of the kingdom.
Hail, through whom trophies are raised,
Hail, through whom enemies fall.
Hail, healing of my flesh,
Hail, salvation of my soul.
Hail, Bride without bridegroom.[23]

Another striking hymn, drawing out the imagery associated with the Mother of God, is the apolytikion for the Forefeast of the Nativity of Christ:

Get ready, Bethlehem, Eden has been opened to all. Rejoice, Ephratha, because the tree of life has blossomed from the Virgin in the cave. For her womb has been shown to be the spiritual paradise, in which is the divine plant; eating of which we shall live, we shall not have died like Adam. Christ is born, raising up the once-fallen image.

Icons of the Virgin Mary, the Mother of God, explore visually the way in which she relates to her son and also to us. Two of the earliest forms depict the Mother of God holding Christ in one arm (usually the left) and pointing to him with her hand (usually the right); this is the Mother of God *Hodigitria*, the one who points to the way to Christ, who is the Way (*hodos* in Greek), the Truth and the Life. Another early form presents the Mother of God seated on a throne holding Christ in her lap; often she is flanked by saints. Again she presents her son to the world for worship and entreaty.

In both these types of icons, the Mother of God is represented as a majestic figure. Later on in the Byzantine period different forms of icons of the Mother of God develop (though often enough there seems to be little correlation between inscriptions on icons and different iconographic types: the Virgin *Hodigitria* can be inscribed *Pammakaristos*, all-blessed, or *Eleousa*, merciful). These include the Virgin *Galaktotrophousa* (the nursing mother), *Glykophilousa* (kissing, or embracing, the infant Christ) and *Eleousa* (merciful, both, I think,

---

[23] *Akathistos Hymn, ikos* 12 in *Orthodox Prayer Book*, 45–6.

looking with compassion on her son who is to die, and with an expression manifesting her mercy towards us). These developments represent the Mother of God more tenderly.

Icons and prayer

Icons came to fulfil a manifold role. From as early as the seventh century, a procession with an icon of the Mother of God became the focus for the prayers offered to her for the protection of the city of Constantinople. This public use of the icon as a kind of paladin continued, and was common throughout Russia. An interesting example of the Russian reception of Byzantine icons of the Mother of God as protector of Christians is the Pokrov icon – pokrov meaning both 'veil' and 'protection'. This relates to an event in the history of the Byzantine Empire, when Constantinople was besieged and the court gathered for prayer in the Vlachernai chapel in the palace. As they were praying, St Andrew the Fool, who was present, saw the Mother of God holding her veil over the city: a sign that it would be preserved. This event was scarcely commemorated in the Byzantine Empire, but became very popular among the Slavs.

But the icons had a more intimate role. Since icons themselves are images, copies of icons, icons of icons, are themselves icons. So whereas at one level there are the great icons of the imperial and princely courts, of great cathedrals, monasteries and places of pilgrimage, at another level copies of these icons were believed to possess the same powers as the originals – and anyway, the real 'originals' are properly speaking the figures depicted: Christ, his divine Mother, and the saints. For it is not as objects of art, where originality might be of some importance, that icons are venerated, but as objects of devotion, as religious objects exercising power through the prayers of those depicted, and invoked, in the icons. Icons brought the 'thinness' of the boundary between heaven and earth into the home itself: in the 'beautiful corner', *krasny ugol*, icons were set up, with lamps burning before them, and members of the household had recourse to them in their prayers. Holiness, and the power of holiness, was never far away.

In 1900, the poet Rainer Maria Rilke visited Russia with his friend, Lou Andreas Salome. The monasteries and churches, the icons and the devotion of the people, made a great impact on him. A few years later he published a collection of poems, *Das Buch der Bilder* (Book of Pictures – or even Book of Icons). It contains a cycle of poems called 'The Tsars'. Towards the end of this cycle, a Tsar, returning home after an unsuccessful campaign, goes into his chapel and kneels before the icon of the Mother of God. The poem continues:

> The two hands, strangely still and brown,
> proclaim that in precious icons,
> there dwells, as in a shrine, majesty
> which overflows from the Son,
> like a drop, within which is discerned
> the azure of the never-to-be-hoped-for, cloudless heavens.

> The hands point to Him;
> but the countenance is like a door
> opening on to the warm light of dusk,
> in which gracious smiles seem with their light
> to wander over her lips, and disappear.

> Then the Tsar bowed down deeply before it, and said:

> Did you not feel the insistent pressure of
> all our feelings, our fears and demands?
> We waited on your dear face,
> that has long gone from us; where has it gone?

> But it does not depart from the great saints.[24]

Rilke could not bring himself to embrace the faith that so attracted him. Nonetheless, it seems to me that he catches the intimacy the Tsar found with the Mother of God, even in disappointment. And even in that disappointment, the Tsar is confident that, though he has lost her gracious regard, this still remains a reality.

It is to that reality – the reality of the tender care of God for human kind, made palpable in the Incarnation, and effective through the prayers and intercessions of the saints, above all the Mother of God herself – that the icons of the Orthodox Church bear witness.

---

[24] Rainer Maria Rilke, 'Die Zaren', section 6, in *Das Buch der Bilder* (Leipzig: Insel-Verlag, 1931), 104–5.

8

Time and the liturgy

Theology and participation

So far we have dealt with the kind of subjects one might expect to find in a course on Eastern Orthodox theology – God, the Trinity, Christology, Creation, Fall, Redemption, Theosis, the Church, the Sacraments, Icons – and in the last chapter we shall look at eschatology. These are all traditional subjects, related, in one way or another, to the faith we confess in the creed. But 'Time and the Liturgy': what kind of a subject is that? It sounds like either something already covered – in the chapter on the Sacraments – or something too metaphysical for a book such as this.

My reason for including this chapter has to do with what I think it means to understand Orthodox theology. For, though there is much to learn about the Orthodox Church and its beliefs – lots of history, lots of complex theological ideas, lots of detail about the liturgy, the way it is celebrated and its meaning, lots about how to live the Christian life in an Orthodox way: rules of fasting, ways of asceticism, and learning to live a life transfigured by God's love – if all this remains at the level of knowledge, information, it is all rather pointless. This is true of any system of belief that issues in a way of life, but it seems to me to be radically true of Orthodoxy. The only knowledge that counts, the only theology that is truly Orthodox, is participation in God's movement in love towards us in creation and Incarnation by our response of love.

St Maximos the Confessor puts this very beautifully in his commentary on the Lord's Prayer, in a passage we have already examined in part in Chapter 2:

> For hidden within a limited compass this prayer contains the whole purpose and aim of which we have just spoken . . . The prayer includes petitions for everything that the divine Word effected through his self-emptying in the Incarnation, and it teaches us to strive for those blessings of which the true provider is God the Father alone through the natural mediation of the Son in the Holy Spirit . . . It was on the

behalf [of human beings] and for their sake that without changing he became man, and is now the author and teacher of so many and such great new mysteries as yet beyond our understanding . . .

Theology is taught us by the incarnate Word of God, since he reveals in himself the Father and the Holy Spirit . . .

The Word bestows adoption on us when he grants us that birth and deification which, transcending nature, come by grace from above through the Spirit. The guarding and preservation of this in God depends on the resolve of those thus born: on their sincere acceptance of the grace bestowed on them and, through the practice of the commandments, on their cultivation of the beauty given to them by grace. Moreover, by emptying themselves of the passions they lay hold of the divine to the same degree as that to which, deliberately emptying himself of his own sublime glory, the Word of God truly became man.

The Word has made men equal to the angels . . .

The Word enables us to participate in divine life by making himself our food, in a manner understood by himself and by those who have received from him a spiritual perception of this kind . . .

He restores human nature to itself . . .

The Word destroys the tyranny of the evil one, who dominates us through deceit, by triumphantly using as a weapon against him the flesh defeated in Adam . . .[1]

The way in which St Maximos understands theology is striking here. First, the mysteries of theology are mediated by a prayer, not by a creed or a treatise: we only understand by participating ourselves in prayer. Second, all that follows is seen in terms of engagement with God, flowing from prayer: accepting God's gifts and using them, even more, imitating in our movement towards God, his movement towards us, so that the Word's *kenosis*, self-emptying, calls forth our self-emptying, and love responds to love: 'deep calls to deep', as the psalmist says (Ps. 41.8).

Participation and the divine liturgy

How do we participate in theology understood like this? Primarily through participation in the divine liturgy, for it is here that the truths

---

[1] Maximos the Confessor, *On the Lord's Prayer*, in *Opuscula exegetica duo* (ed. P. Van Deun; CCSG, 23; Turnhout: Brepols, 1991), 62–164 (Eng. trans. slightly modified, in *The Philokalia: The Complete Text*, vol. 2 [trans. G. E. H. Palmer, Philip Sherrard and Kallistos Ware; London and Boston: Faber & Faber, 1981], 286–9).

that we confess are not just brought to mind, but in some way enacted so that we can take part. But if we say that they are enacted, we are suggesting that there is a process, that something takes place. It is not just a matter of registering them, but taking part in their enactment.

In Dionysios the Areopagite's *Ecclesiastical Hierarchy*, we find an account of the divine liturgy. It begins like this:

> The hierarch, having completed a reverent prayer, near the divine altar, starts with the censing, and proceeds to every part of the enclosure of the sacred place; he then returns to the divine altar and begins the sacred chanting of the psalms . . .[2]

In the next section, the *theoria* or contemplation, he explains this rite of censing thus:

> We must, then, in my opinion, pass within the all-holy mysteries, after we have laid bare the intelligible of the first of the votive gifts, to gaze upon its godlike beauty, and view the hierarch, divinely going with sweet fragrance from the divine altar to the furthermost bounds of the holy place, and again returning to it to complete the function. For the Blessedness, supremely divine above all, even if, through divine goodness, it goes forth to the communion of the holy who participate in it, yet it never goes outside its essential unmoved position and stead-fastness; and illuminates all the godlike in due degree, being always self-centred, and in no wise moved from its own proper identity; so, too, the divine initiation of the synaxis, although it has a unique, and simple, and enfolded source, is multiplied, out of love towards mankind, into the holy variety of the symbols, and travels through the whole range of the supremely divine description; yet uniformly it is again collected from these, into its own proper monad, and unifies those who are being reverently conducted towards it. In the same godlike manner, the divine hierarch, if he benignly lowers to his subordinates his own unique hierarchical science, by using the multiplicities of the holy enigmas, yet again, as absolute, and not to be held in check by smaller things, he is restored to his proper headship without diminution, and, when he has made the intellectual entry of himself to the One, he sees clearly the uniform principles of things accomplished, as he makes the goal of his philanthropic progress to things secondary the more divine return to things primary.[3]

---

[2] *EH* 3. 2.
[3] *EH* 3. 3. 3.

The censing of the Church at the beginning of the liturgy, which still takes place, is seen by Dionysios as symbolic of the movement in love of the One into the realm of the many and back to the One itself: the One moves out into the realm of the manifold, and embraces it, and draws it back into the primordial union. It is a circular movement. Dionysios is at pains to emphasize that, though it is a genuine movement, through love, into the realm of the manifold, the One does not desert its own unity, so there is no danger of the circular movement drifting off into cycles of multiplicity. Dionysios understands this circular movement in terms of the Neoplatonic triad of rest–procession–return, a fundamental circular movement underlying all reality. Beings with reason and consciousness of themselves are capable of participating in this movement actively, rather than simply being caught up in a fundamental characteristic of reality, the eternal cycle of rest–procession–return; they participate in it with awareness through contemplation, through a loving gaze towards the still centre from which they derive.

It seems to me that this circular movement is a powerful symbol for many aspects of what is involved in participating in God's movement towards us in creation and Incarnation through which he draws us back into union with himself. Awareness of this helps us to grasp what is happening in our participation in the divine liturgy.

Time and space – cycles of change

And time? It is often said that there are two conceptions of time – one cyclic and the other linear; one conceives of time either as consisting of recurring cycles, or as something that moves in a linear way from the past to the future. It was popular, among theologians of the last century, to oppose these two notions of time and see the cyclical as in some sense Greek or pagan, in contrast to linear time, moving into the future, which was regarded as biblical. This seems to me an oversimplification, for cyclical ways of understanding time are as much a part of the biblical concept as the sense of a linear movement from creation to consummation. For it is through various cycles, which repeat themselves, that we grasp the passage of time. The day, the month, the year: these are cycles related to the circular movement of the earth, the moon and the sun, or, as the ancients would have thought of it, the sun, the moon and the sphere of the fixed stars. For it was the movement of the sun round the earth that was thought to determine the day, the revolution of the moon round the earth that determined the month (as we still conceive it) and the revolution of the sphere of the fixed stars that determined the year.

There are other cycles associated with these fundamental cycles. The year, for instance, is broken down in the sequence of the seasons: spring, summer, autumn and winter. The Jewish tradition, as we find it in the Scriptures, adds another cycle: the cycle of the week, consisting of seven days from Sunday to Saturday. Famously, these various cycles do not fit into each other in any tidy way: the month is a bit more than four weeks; the year a bit more than 12 lunar months. It is this that makes the calendar a complicated business; for centuries an enormous amount of human ingenuity has gone into bringing these cycles into some sort of conjunction.

There are two ways of doing this, and the Christian calendar incorporates both of them. The Julian calendar, adopted by the Christians of the Roman Empire, is one way of bringing the solar year and the lunar year into conjunction (I am going to use our modern way of referring to these, though I suppose, historically, I should say the sidereal year): the 12 months of the lunar year are extended by two or three days (except for February) so that the 12 months encompass 365 days. This means that the months are no longer lunar; the full moon shifts about each month, and one can even have two moons in a single calendar month; lunar time is, if you like, subordinated to solar time.

The Christian Church, however, remained attached to the lunar year, for one reason: the celebration of Easter, or Pascha, the Christian Passover. As the name 'Pascha' suggests, the Christian feast is based on the Jewish Passover, Pesach, or Pasch. The way the Hebrews worked out the date of Passover involved bringing lunar and solar time into some kind of conjunction. For the Jews, like the Muslims who follow them in this, have a year of 12 lunar months, though, unlike the Muslims, every so often an extra lunar month is intercalated, so that the Jewish year corresponds roughly to the solar year, and the months relate to the seasons of the year. Passover was held on 14 Nisan, the date of the full moon after the spring equinox. Based on that, Christians by the end of the second century determined Easter as the Sunday after the first full moon after the spring equinox (as the equinox was judged to be

21 March, Easter could occur on any date between 22 March and 25 April). This brings into conjunction three of the cycles mentioned: the week, the (lunar) month and the (solar) year. Easter is the first day of the week (Sunday), occurring in the middle of the lunar month, after the full moon, in spring, the season in which the earth comes to life.

The revolution of these cycles – their conjunction and disjunction – gives shape to the sequence of time, which would otherwise be – as it has perhaps largely become in the secular West – a sequence of indistinguishable days. Let us start with the day: in the Orthodox calendar (as in the Western calendar on feast days, until the Vatican II reforms) the day starts in the evening with the setting of the sun – in Genesis each day is described as 'evening and morning' – and moves through to the light of the morning; the day moves from darkness to light, ultimately towards the 'light without evening' of the kingdom of heaven. Then the week, which starts with Sunday, the day of the resurrection; in Russian it is called *Voskresene*, 'resurrection', in Greek, *Kyriaki*, the Lord's Day, as it has also been called in England. In an odd way the week also ends with Sunday, the eighth day, coming full cycle on that day (the Orthodox lectionary of scriptural readings, for example, is organized in terms of weeks that end on Sunday): again pointing to the eighth day, the symbol of the 'day without evening' of the kingdom. The sequence of lunar cycles (or months) also begins with the paschal full moon, and the various seasons of the year are reflected in the festivals of the Church Year.

The Church Year – cycles of time

Easter is the central turning point in the Christian Year. It is preceded by the great 40-day fast of Lent. There developed different ways of interpreting this fast. In the West the 40 days are counted back from Holy Saturday, omitting Sundays, so that Lent begins on Ash Wednesday; in the East the 40-day period begins on Clean Monday (two days before Ash Wednesday, when Easters coincide) and ends on the weekend before Easter – with Lazarus Saturday (commemorating the raising of Lazarus) and the Entry of Christ into Jerusalem on Palm Sunday ushering in Great and Holy Week. Easter is followed by the 50 days leading up to Pentecost (which means 'fiftieth [day]'), by way of the Feast of the Ascension, 40 days after Easter. So there is a period of nearly three months in the Christian calendar determined by the paschal full moon, and the dates connected with it are detached, as it were, from the solar year of 12 months.

For most of the year, the feasts and fasts of the Church are determined by the solar year, but for the three months from the beginning of Lent until the end of the paschal season, they follow the lunar year which determines Easter. The feasts of the solar year are called fixed feasts; those determined by the date of Easter moveable feasts.

The solar year itself, beginning in January and ending in December, is marked by various celebrations: first of all, the celebrations of the feasts of the martyrs, and later other saints, generally on the date of their martyrdom, their 'heavenly birthday'. The notion of the Church Year is more closely linked to the Roman year than in the West, where the Church Year begins with the first Sunday of Advent, four Sundays before Christmas. Although the year begins on 1 January, the Feast of Christ's circumcision and also of St Basil the Great, one of the great fourth-century Fathers of the Church, properly speaking the Church Year is considered to begin on 1 September, the beginning of the Indiction (the Byzantine tax year!). This day is now dedicated to prayer for the environment, and also to the Feast of the great saint of the fifth century, St Symeon the Stylite, or Pillar Saint.

In addition to the feasts of the martyrs, there are various fixed feasts with calendrical dates related to the lives of Christ and the Virgin Mary, the Mother of God. It is clearest if we think of these in terms of cycles.

There is a cycle associated with Christ, based on events recorded in the Gospels and focusing on the Feast of the Nativity of Christ, celebrated on 25 December. This is a much later feast than Easter, which goes back as early as we have evidence. The first evidence for a feast celebrating the nativity of Christ is found in the fourth century, and by the end of the century this celebration occurs on two dates: 25 December and 6 January. The date observed in Rome and the West seems to have been 25 December, while in the East it was 6 January that was observed, as a feast celebrating not just the physical birth of Christ, but his manifestation in the world, both in his birth and at the beginning of his earthly ministry in his baptism by John the Baptist and in his first miracle at Cana in Galilee, where water was changed into wine.

By the end of the century, East and West became aware of each other's practice and sought to incorporate both feasts. They did this in different ways. The West chose 25 December on which to celebrate the birth of Christ in the manger, and 6 January to celebrate his manifestation to the Wise Men (and also, subordinately, his baptism and the miracle at Cana in Galilee – this is clear, even in the post-Vatican II office, where the antiphon for the Magnificat at Vespers reads: 'We celebrate this holy day adorned by three miracles: today a star led the magi to the manger; today water was changed into wine at the wedding; today in the Jordan Christ willed to be baptized by John, to save us, alleluia!'). The East probably followed the liturgical custom of Jerusalem and the Holy Land – many liturgical customs in the East can be traced back to the practice in Jerusalem – where biblical feasts were celebrated at the holy sites, so that 25 December was assigned to Bethlehem and the celebration of the nativity of Christ, with the worship of both shepherds and magi, while 6 January was assigned to the River Jordan, with the celebration of the baptism of Christ. (Cana was far away in Galilee, and so maybe slipped out of the loop.)

The next feast in the cycle associated with Christ is, as we have seen, the Feast of Theophany or Epiphany: the manifestation of Christ to the world. For the East this is his manifestation as God, and with that manifestation the revelation of the Trinity: as the troparion puts it,

> As you were baptized in the Jordan, Lord, the worship of the Trinity was made manifest, for the voice of the Father bore witness to you, naming you the beloved Son; and the Spirit in the form of a dove confirmed the sureness of the word. Christ God, who appeared and enlightened the world, glory to You![4]

There are other feasts associated with Christmas. The Feast of the Annunciation to the Mother of God takes place on 25 March, nine months before Christmas, and 40 days after, on 2 February, is the Feast of the Meeting of Christ in the Temple (in the West, the Purification of the Virgin Mary or the Presentation), when he was taken there on the fortieth day in accordance with the Hebrew law. On 6 August the Feast of the Transfiguration of Christ is celebrated, and on 14 September the Feast of the Exaltation of the Cross. There is a cycle consisting of the Exaltation of the Cross–Christmas–Theophany–the Meeting of Christ in the Temple–the Annunciation,

---

[4] *An Orthodox Prayer Book* (Eng. trans. Archimandrite Ephrem Lash; Milton under Wychwood: Fellowship of St Alban & St Sergius, 2009), 102.

and then the paschal cycle – Palm Sunday, Easter, Ascension and Pentecost – and finally the Transfiguration.

There is another cycle associated with the life of the Mother of God. This cycle is drawn not from the canonical Gospels, but from apocryphal writings, the so-called *Protevangelium of James* and the accounts of the dormition and assumption of the Mother of God. The *Protevangelium* is a second-century account of the life of the Virgin up to the massacre of the innocents. It is a remarkable text, full of symbolism. As we have already noticed, it is here we find the story that, at the annunciation, the Virgin was spinning the scarlet and purple thread for the veil of the Temple, the veil that would be rent asunder at the crucifixion, and the account of Joseph, going in search of a midwife, after finding a cave for the Virgin, and as Christ is born, finding that time stands still:

> But I, Joseph, was walking, and I was not walking. I looked up to the vault of heaven, and saw it standing still . . . I looked down at the torrential stream, and I saw some goats whose mouths were over the water, but they were not drinking. Then suddenly everything returned to its normal course.[5]

The *Protevangelium* yields the Feasts of the Nativity of the Mother of God on 8 September, and of her Entry into the Temple on 21 November. The Feast of her Dormition on 15 August, drawn too from apocryphal accounts,[6] was decreed a feast of the Byzantine Empire by Emperor Maurice at the end of the sixth century. (There is also a Feast of her Conception, celebrated on 9 December.) This Marian cycle meshes with the Christ cycle in that feasts such as the Annunciation, Christmas, the Meeting of Christ in the Temple, Ascension and Pentecost, also involve the Mother of God. We have, then, two cycles – of Christ and of his Virgin Mother – that are nested one in another. Together they constitute the Twelve Great Feasts – beginning in the Church Year with the Feast of the Nativity of the Mother of God on 8 September and ending with the Feast of her Dormition on 15 August – plus the Feast of Pascha, the 'Feast of Feasts'.

---

[5] *Prot.* 18.2. See *The Apocryphal Gospels* (texts and trans. Bart D. Ehrman and Zlatko Plešu; Oxford: Oxford University Press, 2011), 61.
[6] On which, see Stephen J. Shoemaker, *Ancient Traditions of the Virgin Mary's Dormition and Assumption* (Oxford: Oxford University Press, 2002).

There are feasts, but also fasts. In the week, each Sunday is a Feast of the Resurrection, and Wednesday and Friday are fasts, a practice first recorded in the *Didache* (*Did.* 8.1). In the year the 50 days from Easter to Pentecost constitute one long feast, and the 40 days of Lent, plus Holy Week, constitute one long fast (mitigated on Saturdays and Sundays, because of the weekly celebration of the resurrection). However, in the course of the year there have developed other periods of fasting: the 40 days before Christmas (sometimes called the St Philip Fast, as it begins on 15 November, the day after the Feast of St Philip the Apostle); the period between the final end of the Easter season, the Sunday after Pentecost, the Sunday of All Saints, and the Feast of the Apostles Peter and Paul (on 29 June); and the first 14 days of August before the Feast of the Dormition on the 15th. Feasts and fasts give shape to the year, providing periods of preparation by fasting for the periods in which we celebrate the key points in the history of salvation, continued in the celebrations of the martyrs and saints.

In the Church Year, therefore, we have a conjunction of cycles that shape the year and enable us to move through the various elements constituting the events that add up to the engagement between God and humanity that culminated in the Incarnation.

Cycles – of meaning or unmeaning

The notion of time as cyclical can be regarded from different perspectives. Plato saw time, *chronos*, as a 'moving image of eternity' (*Timaeus* 37d), manifest in the circular movement of the heavens. The circular movement gave shape to the movement that characterizes the life of finite beings, focusing that movement on the stillness that lies at the heart of reality and reflected in the calm circlings of the stars. The Welsh poet, Henry Vaughan, caught something of this in his poem, 'The World':

> I saw Eternity the other night
> Like a great *Ring* of pure and endless light,
>   All calm, as it was bright,
> And round beneath it, Time in hours, days, years
>   Driv'n by the spheres
> Like a vast shadow mov'd, In which the world
>   And all her train were hurl'd . . .

The rest of the poem is mostly concerned with those who cannot see eternity, this 'ring of pure and endless light', but are trapped in dark cycles that draw them down away from the light: the statesman, the miser, the epicure. For the notion of the cyclical is ambiguous: we can use the image of cyclical movement to capture a sense of meaninglessness, or of a vortex that sucks us down, overpowering us. T. S. Eliot called April the 'cruellest month', because it is a month of fresh beginnings, new shoots that spring up full of hope, a hope that will be exhausted come winter. It ushers in a cycle of meaninglessness, a cycle in which signs of hope are mocked. This sense of a cycle of meaninglessness is very powerful; the sense that we are caught in revolutions that entrap us and bring us round and round to the same thing, making no kind of advance – all this is very familiar. The cycles of the liturgical celebration of the Church – daily, weekly, monthly, yearly – are ways in which the cycles of meaninglessness in which we find ourselves too often trapped can be redeemed and find meaning.

The symbolism of the liturgy

How does this happen? Essentially through the symbolism we have already looked at: symbolism that relates the temporal to the eternal, and sees the material as embodying the spiritual. Such symbols are found throughout creation, but are focused in the symbolism of the sacraments and icons that we explored in the last chapter. This symbolism is gathered up in the worship of the Orthodox Church, in the symbolism of the church building and the services and ceremonies and even gestures that take place within it, and the way these all fit into the cycles of celebration we find in the days and the weeks of the Church's Year, and what might think of as the nested cycles that are contained in it. In the early chapters of his work *The Mystagogia*, St Maximos the Confessor sets up the structures that contain and express the meaning of the Church and what takes place in it. He begins by discussing how the Church may be seen as 'an image and type of God' by imitating and representing God's activity (*energeia*). God has brought everything into being, 'contains, gathers and limits them and in his providence binds both intelligible and sensible beings to himself and one another'. It is in this way that the holy Church of God will be shown to be active among us in the same way as God, as an image reflects its archetype. For many and of nearly boundless number are the men, women and children who are distinct from one another and vastly different by birth and appearance, by race and language, by way of life and age, by opinions and skills, by manners and customs, by pursuits and studies, and still again by reputation, fortune, characteristics and habits: all are born into the Church and through it are reborn and recreated in the Spirit. To all in equal measures it gives and bestows one divine form and designation, to be Christ's and to carry his name. In accordance with faith it gives to all a single, simple, whole and indivisible condition which does not allow us to bring to mind the existence of the myriads of differences among them, even if they do exist, through the universal relationship and union of all things with it. It is through it that absolutely no one at all is in himself separated from the community since everyone converges with all the rest and joins together with them by the one, simple, and indivisible grace and power of faith. 'For all', it is said, 'had but one heart and one mind'. Thus to be and to appear as one body formed of different members is really worthy of Christ himself, our true head, in whom says the divine Apostle, 'there is neither male nor female, neither Jew nor Greek, neither circumcision nor uncircumcision, neither barbarian nor Scythian, neither slave nor free, but he is all and in all'. It is he who encloses in himself all beings by the unique, simple and infinitely wise power of his goodness.[7]

Maximos goes on to apply the analogy of the radii of a circle converging on the centre to both God's relationship to the created order and the Church's relationship to its members, and concludes that, in both cases, there is achieved a union that, though profound, does not confuse the beings joined, but preserves their integrity.

In the chapters that follow Maximos shows how the union of differences found in the Church is also reflected throughout the created order. To begin with, he suggests that the Church may be seen as an image of the cosmos, regarded as made up of visible and invisible beings. He has now moved to thinking of the church as a building, and more precisely as a building divided into two: the area for 'the priests and ministers alone', that is, the sanctuary (in Greek: *hierateion*), and the area for the 'all the faithful people', which is called

---

[7] *Mystagogia* 1. 163–89 (ed. Christian Boudignon; CCSG 69; Turnbout: Brepols, 2011), my translation.

the nave (*naon*).[8] This distinction he finds echoed in the cosmos, in the distinction there between the invisible part of the cosmos and the visible part. These two parts are closely related; indeed, Maximos says, the church is not properly speaking divided by the differences between the two parts, but rather by the relationship between the two parts, so that,

> the nave is potentially the sanctuary since it is a holy place by reason of its relationship to the goal of sacred initiation (or: mystagogy), and the sanctuary is actually the nave, since it is there that the process of its own sacred initiation begins.[9]

So, too, with the cosmos:

> for the whole intelligible cosmos is imprinted in a hidden way on the whole sensible cosmos through the symbolic forms, while the whole sensible cosmos can be understood to be present to the intelligible cosmos through its principles (*logoi*) that reveal its simplicity to the intellect.[10]

The distinction found in cosmos and Church that makes the one an image of the other is matter of relationship rather than separation; it is a matter of connexion, and not division. And it is an ordered connexion, the visible pointing to the invisible realm, so that the visible finds its meaning in the invisible, and the invisible finds its expression in the visible, in this way reflecting the close relationship between sanctuary and nave in the church.

The following chapters suggest further images of the Church: in the visible world itself, consisting as it does of heaven and earth (chapter 3), and then in the human person, consisting of body and soul (chapter 4) and the soul, consisting of soul and intellect (chapter 5). Chapters 4 and 5 develop a fairly detailed understanding of the spiritual life. They move from the level of body, which is the level of ascetic struggle, in which we learn moral wisdom, to the level of soul, which is the level of natural contemplation, that is

---

[8] It is worth noting that, in speaking of the Church, first, Maximos does not use any technical term for the unordained laity (such as the already well-established term, *laïkos*), but instead refers to 'all the faithful people', and second, *naos* means a temple, that is the whole building (and is still used in that sense), so that the distinction is really between the building as a whole and a special part of it, and analogously for the community.

[9] *Mystagogia* 2. 221–4 (ed. Boudignon, my translation).

[10] *Mystagogia* 2. 241–4 (ed. Boudignon, my translation).

contemplation of the principles (*logoi*) of the cosmos, which are all summed up in the *Logos* himself, Christ. Finally we reach the level of intellect, the level of mystical theology, that is contemplation of God himself (Maximos, while still using the image of the twofold church to interpret the passage from one level to another, also combines them in a threefold image of the church with nave, sanctuary and altar, *thusiasterion*). Chapter 6 introduces a further image of the Church:

> just as, in accordance with contemplation that brings about ascent, he [the 'old man', or *geronta*, to whom Maximos attributes his *Mystagogia*] called the Church a spiritual human being and human kind a mystical Church, so he said that the whole of holy Scripture is, in short, a human being, the Old Testament having the body, and the New Testament soul and spirit and intellect, or again, taking the whole of holy Scripture, both Old and New Testaments, its body is the historical letter, while the meaning of what is written and its purpose, towards which the intellect strives, is the soul.[11]

The purpose of all these interlinking images seems to be manifold. It means that anything that takes place in one context has its counterpart in another, so that the meaning of everything that takes place in any of these contexts both borrows from and contributes to the others. There are then profound interconnections between Church, cosmos (understood both as embracing the spiritual and material realm and as embracing the visible heavens and the earth), the inward life of the human person and even the Scriptures themselves. This means that the Church and what happens in it has implications for the cosmos, but also implications that reach into the heart of each individual Christian and his or her own pilgrimage towards union with God; it means, too, that the Church, like Scripture, is a place where God has made himself known, and this being made known is not just, or even, a matter of information, but rather a matter of participation in God himself through his activities or energies.

'He placed Himself in the order of signs':[12] these words from the early twentieth-century Catholic theologian, Maurice de la Taille,

---

[11] *Mystagogia* 6. 507–14 (ed. Boudignon, my translation).

[12] Maurice de la Taille SJ, *The Mystery of Faith and Human Opinion Contrasted and Defined* (London: Sheed & Ward, 1934), 212.

seemed to David Jones the key to the way in which the sacramental principle is effected. What Christ did in the paschal mystery and continues to do in the recalling, *anamnesis*, of this in the Eucharist has resonances that reach into the heart of the individual Christian and into the structures of the created order, the cosmos. All this is invoked in lines with which his great poetic cycle, *The Anathemata*, reaches its end:

> He does what is done in many places
> what he does other
>   he does after the mode
> of what has always been done.
> What did he do other
>   recumbent at the garnished supper?
> What did he do yet other
>   riding the Axile Tree?[13]

Already by Maximos' time in the seventh century, the church building was conceived as a little cosmos, just as the human being is in the teaching of the Fathers. In the succeeding centuries this became more and more manifest. The church building evolved to acquire a central dome, within which was depicted Christ Pantokrator, the ruler of all, gazing down from heaven to the people gathered on earth. Heaven, however, appeared not just above, but ahead, for the sanctuary – or altar – separated from the nave by a screen, represents heaven, as we recall from Maximos' series of images. The screen, over the centuries, became more and more elaborate, so that nowadays the screen, the iconostasis, consists of rows of icons, depicting Christ, the Mother of God and the saints, who, as it were, gaze at us from the threshold of heaven. In the altar itself there is generally an apse in which is depicted the Mother of God, for the Mother of God is regarded as a living Temple, in which God dwelt in order to become human, and who shows us Christ and draws us to him.

The representation of heaven, both above and ahead, combines, as it were, the sense of time as both cyclical and linear. The experience of time in the Church is a 'moving image of eternity' – eternity represented in the dome – and as well a movement from the nave to the sanctuary, from earth to heaven, a movement that meets God's movement to us in the Incarnation.

---

[13] David Jones, *The Anathemata* (2nd edn; London: Faber & Faber, 1955), 243.

Much of the symbolism of the liturgical services underlines all this. There is movement from the sanctuary to the nave – pre-eminently the Little Entrance with the Gospel in the divine liturgy or with incense at Vespers, and the Great Entrance with the holy gifts. The deacon, too, comes out from the sanctuary to sing the litanies, to bring before God the needs of those in the church, and then returns into the sanctuary. Moving between sanctuary and nave, heaven and earth, the deacon is compared to the angels, and his free-flowing stole or orarion is understood as a symbol of his freedom.[14] Generally when the priest appears at the holy doors in the centre of the iconostasis, it is to give a blessing: Peace to all! The wishing of peace was an ancient Jewish greeting, and you can still hear the greeting 'Shalom' in the streets of Jerusalem. Yet for Christians it has a more precise significance: it is the greeting of the risen Christ in the Gospels, and the priest's, or the bishop's, greeting, 'Peace to all', recalls that.

There are other aspects of the liturgical services that recall the resurrection, not least the recitation after communion in the Russian tradition of various verses relating to the resurrection, leading into the beginning of the ninth ode at Easter Matins – 'Shine, shine, O New Jerusalem' – and ending with the verse: 'Christ, great and most holy Passover! Wisdom and Word and Power of God! Grant that we may partake of you more fully in the day without evening of your kingdom.' For it is the resurrection that makes the difference, that makes possible the transformation of the death-dealing cycles of fallen life into the round dance of the resurrection.

Liturgical dance

Outside the divine liturgy of the Eucharist, there are three occasions when there takes place in church what is actually called a dance – a dance that involves a circling movement widdershins, or anti-clockwise – and those occasions are baptism, the wedding service and ordination. (In the latter two cases it is called the Dance of Isaias, because one of the troparia sung invokes the prophet Isaias and uses words from his prophecy of the Virgin Birth [Isa. 7.14].) In the

---

[14] See Theodore of Mopsuestia, *Homily* 15. 23, in *Les Homélies catéchétiques de Théodore de Mopsueste* (ed. Raymond Tonneau OP and Robert Devreesse; Studi e Testi, 145; Rome: Biblioteca Apostolica Vaticana, 1949), 501.

case of baptism and the wedding service the dance takes place in the nave, around the font or a table set out in the church; in the case of ordination, the dance takes place round the holy table in the sanctuary.

In her book on the symbolic significance of the ceremonies of a Greek village, *Cosmos, Life, and Liturgy in a Greek Orthodox Village*, Juliet du Boulay points out how the round dance that is such a feature on many occasions in village life reflects the circular movements in the Church's liturgy, so that each is taken into the other. The dance in the village relates the concerns of everyday life to the services in the Church and the cycles in the Church – in the ceremonies and in the cycles of the day, the month, the year – giving meaning and healing to the marred nature of fallen life. Dr du Boulay has this to say:

> The fallen world, then, is a living presence alongside the unfallen one; but it is felt to be possible at any time to make a reconnection with the timeless world beyond this middle ground of the cosmos and of time, and this in turn brings about a series of radical transformations.
>
> The action which is felt to reconnect with this timeless world, and to transform the doomed cycle of the fallen world, has been described again and again in the typical sayings of the villagers. It is the move-ment away from the evil choice towards the good, away from the devil and towards Christ, from the fallen consciousness and towards the paradisal one. This movement of the Church's liturgy further defines as being from the remorseless sequence of cause and effect, sin and punishment, power and subjection, fate and suffering, which are locked together in the linear stream of this world's time, and towards the potentialities of the present moment, 'Today'. For in the eternal 'Today', the liberating energies of the risen Christ, and the intercession of the holy figures of the Church who have already been sanctified by him, can draw the powerless, the sinner, and the fated back into the divine world.[15]

'At any time', 'today': this very moment – the 'today' of the liturgical action, in which we find ourselves present, fundamentally at the paschal mystery – the death and resurrection of Christ – but also at all the moments of sacred time that we celebrate in the course of the

---

[15] Juliet du Boulay, *Cosmos, Life, and Liturgy in a Greek Orthodox Village* (Limni, Greece: D. Harvey, 2009), 400.

Christian Year. So it is that many of the songs for the great feasts begin 'today':

- at the Entry of the Mother of God: 'Today is the prelude of the good pleasure of God . . . In the Temple of God the Virgin is revealed . . .';
- at Christmas: 'Today the Virgin gives birth to him who is above all being, and the earth offers a cave to him whom no one can approach . . .';
- at Theophany (in the West, Epiphany): 'Today you have appeared to the inhabited world . . . You have come, you have appeared, the unapproachable Light';
- at the Annunciation: 'Today is the crowning moment of our salvation, and the unfolding of the eternal mystery: the Son of God becomes the Son of the Virgin . . .'[16]

This sense of an eternal present, not so much the re-enacting of the saving events celebrated, but rather our finding ourselves in the presence of these events, is realized throughout the divine liturgy, especially at the reading of the Gospel, when the deacon reads from the Gospel Book, symbolizing Christ himself, and here and now as we stand in church we listen to the words of the Saviour. This reaches its culmination in the eucharistic prayer, or the anaphora, in which, at the invocation of the Holy Spirit, we find ourselves present with the risen Christ, and in the holy gifts receive his sacred body and precious blood. Here we find ourselves restored to the source of life, receiving the 'heavenly and awesome mysteries . . . with a pure conscience, for forgiveness of sins and pardon of offences, for communion of the Holy Spirit, for inheritance of the kingdom of heaven, and for boldness before you, not for judgment or condemnation'.[17]

I would go one step further, in this presentation of Orthodox theology, and suggest that beyond all the obvious ways of testing the truth of Orthodox doctrine – conformity with the sacred Scriptures, with the witness of the Holy Fathers, with the creeds, with the dogmas proclaimed at the Œcumenical Councils of the Church – there is

---

[16] *Orthodox Prayer Book*, 101, 102, 103, 103–4.
[17] *The Divine Liturgy of our Father among the Saints John Chrysostom* (Oxford: Oxford University Press, 1995), 38–9.

another, more immediate test: Does what we believe find its counter-part in the way we pray in the divine liturgy? It is a simple test, but an immediate one: for the doctrine of the Trinity, of the Incarnation, of human sin and our need for redemption, the victory of the cross and the grace of the resurrection, forgiveness and repentance, love and deification, the intercession of the saints and especially of the Mother of God – all these are present in the prayers we offer in the liturgy, present not just as doctrines but as truths that express the mystery in which we participate through the prayer of the Church, with the divine liturgy at its heart.

9

Where are we going? The last things and eternal life[1]

'He is coming in glory to judge the living and the dead, and his kingdom will have no end'; 'I await the resurrection of the dead, and the life of the age to come'. Despite the fact that, in the doctrine of 'the last things', *ta eschata*, the whole of Christian doctrine – Creation, Incarnation, redemption and deification – finds its fulfilment, there is little explicitly defined in the formularies of the Orthodox Church, hardly anything more than these two phrases of the Nicene Creed. Nevertheless, there is nothing bleakly agnostic about Orthodox beliefs concerning afterlife, nor is awareness of an eschatological dimension absent. Rather, these beliefs are expressed primarily in the rich liturgical life of the Orthodox Church, which is nourished on the hopes and longings of the Scriptures, and, in the case of the last things particularly, on the experiences and insights of the saints, especially as found in their lives and writings. At the centre of all this – the liturgical experience, the Scriptures as understood by the Orthodox and the transfigured lives and experience of the saints – stands the resurrection of Christ, the ultimate fount of Christian hope.

The role of liturgy and saints' lives in shaping Orthodox convictions concerning eschatology is not unlike the case of veneration of the Blessed Virgin Mary, the Mother of God. There, too, the dogmatic data are limited and largely indirect, and devotion to the Mother of God has been nourished by her role in the liturgical cycle of services as a whole, as well as by the liturgical feasts specifically devoted to her, which have drawn, as we have seen, on imaginative accounts of her life in the apocryphal literature: the equivalent in this case of hagiography. In both cases, there have emerged the same dangers:

---

[1] Much of the material in this chapter can be found in my article, 'Eastern Orthodox Eschatology', in *The Oxford Handbook of Eschatology* (ed. Jerry L. Walls; Oxford and New York: Oxford University Press, 2008), 233–47.

the itch to define (which has, perhaps, been more characteristic of the West) and, not always distinct from this, the risk of reading too literally the imaginative exuberance of apocryphal and hagiographical texts.

Fr Sergii Bulgakov, in the section devoted to eschatology in the final volume of his major theological trilogy, *On Divine Wisdom and Godmanhood*, identified these dangers as 'rationalism' and 'anthropomorphism'. Rationalism, he remarked, is often 'anthropomorphism in thought', submitting to the familiar canons of human reasoning mysteries that lie beyond our fallen experience of space and time, while anthropomorphism tends to prevent eschatology from

> being what it is and what it should be, ontology and anthropology revealed in the final destinies of man. The ontological statement of the problem is replaced by a juridical one, and the mysteries of God's love are measured according to the penal code.[2]

In relation to individual eschatology (that is, the fate and state of the individual person after death), a further danger of anthropomorphism is to see the afterlife as a continuation after death of the life of the soul envisaged in much the same terms as this life (that is, in terms of existing under space and time), thereby running the risk of reducing Christian doctrine to mythology.

The centre of the Christian hope, then, is the resurrection of Christ. Christian experience of this finds its pre-eminent expression in participation in the paschal mystery of Christ's death and resurrection through the celebration of the Holy Eucharist, the divine liturgy.

Eucharist as eschatology

From the beginning, the Eucharist has had an eschatological dimension.[3] At the Last Supper, after giving the apostles the wine as his 'blood of the covenant', the Lord said, 'I tell you, I will not drink again of this fruit of the vine, until I drink with you anew in the kingdom of my Father' (Matt. 26.29). In doing what Christ asked his

---

[2] Sergius Bulgakov, *The Bride of the Lamb* (trans. Boris Jakim; Grand Rapids, MI: Eerdmans, 2002), 382; for general discussion referred to, see 381–2.

[3] See Metropolitan John [Zizioulas] of Pergamon, 'The Eucharist and the Kingdom of God', *Sourozh* 58 (November 1994), 1–12; 59 (February 1995), 22–38; 60 (May 1995), 32–46 (trans. Elizabeth Theokritoff from the Greek original).

disciples to do, the Church has 'proclaimed the Lord's death, until he comes' (1 Cor. 11.26). The Eucharist, then, is celebrated as an anticipation of the banquet of the kingdom, that will take place after the second coming of Christ. In gathering together, the early Christians looked forward to the coming of the kingdom; as they celebrated the Eucharist together, they knew themselves to be on the threshold of the kingdom. So in the *Didache*, Christians were exhorted to pray:

> As this fragment [of bread] was scattered over the mountains and has been gathered together into one, so let your Church be gathered from the ends of the world into your kingdom; for yours is the glory and the power through Jesus Christ to the ages. (*Did.* 9.4)

This eschatological dimension has been preserved in the Orthodox liturgy. It begins with the proclamation: 'Blessed is the kingdom of the Father and the Son and the Holy Spirit, now and forever, and to the ages of ages. Amen'; at the Great Entrance, there are prayers to the Lord for all present 'to be remembered in his kingdom'; before the holy gifts are brought out for communion, the Lord's Prayer is prayed, with its petition: 'Your kingdom come!'; and immediately before communion one of the prayers ends with the words: 'but like the Thief I confess you: Remember me, O Lord, in your kingdom'. This repeated recalling of the kingdom preserves the eschatological dimension of the Eucharist; in the liturgy, as we recall the life and teaching, the death and resurrection of Christ, as we receive his sacred body and precious blood, we find ourselves on the threshold of the kingdom, already partaking by anticipation in the banquet of the kingdom.

The eschatological dimension is underlined in other ways. St Maximos the Confessor, in his commentary on the divine liturgy, *The Mystagogia*, interprets the bishop's entry into the church (with which the Eucharist then began) as symbolizing the coming of Christ into the world at the Incarnation. The immediate purpose of the Incarnation in reconciling heaven and earth is symbolized by the readings and the ceremonies that accompany them, and after the proclamation of the Gospel the bishop descends from his throne in an action symbolizing the second coming of Christ. Everything that follows – the reciting of the creed, the offering of bread and wine, consecration and communion – takes place, symbolically, after the second coming of Christ. This is confirmed by the prayer of anamnesis in which remembrance is made of 'this our Saviour's command and all that has been done for us: the Cross, the Tomb, the Resurrection on the third day, the Ascension into heaven, the Sitting at the right hand, the Second and glorious Coming again'.[4] At the heart of the paschal mystery, the Church is beyond time, and looks back, as it were, on the second coming, at the same time as it prays 'Your kingdom come'!

This eschatological orientation of the liturgy spills over into the daily prayer life of the Orthodox Christian who is still expected to follow the custom of the early Church of praying facing east and standing upright, especially on Sundays. St Basil the Great explains this custom thus:

> For this reason we all look to the East during our prayers . . . because we seek our ancient fatherland, paradise, which God planted towards the East. It is standing upright that we make our prayers on the first day of the week . . . It is not only because risen together with Christ, we ought to seek the things above, and through our standing up for prayer on the day of the resurrection call to mind the grace given to us, but because it is a kind of image of the age to come . . . And this one day is also the eighth, pointing to that really unique and truly eighth day . . . the condition that follows our time, the day that will never end, without evening or tomorrow, the imperishable age that will never grow old . . .[5]

St John Damascene recapitulates this tradition, adding that

> also, when the Lord was crucified, he looked towards the West, and so we worship gazing towards him. And when he was taken up, he ascended towards the East and thus the apostles worshipped him and thus he shall come in the same way as they had seen him going into heaven . . . And so, while we are awaiting him, we worship towards the East.[6]

This eschatological orientation of Orthodox prayer and worship has several consequences for more general eschatological considerations. The 'last things' are not remote future events, but events made present in

---

[4] *The Divine Liturgy of our Father among the Saints St John Chrysostom* (Oxford: Oxford University Press, 1995), 33.

[5] *On the Holy Spirit* 27.66. My translation. Cf. St Basil the Great, *On the Holy Spirit* (trans. Stephen Hildebrand; Crestwood, NY: St Vladimir's Seminary Press, 2011), 106.

[6] *Exposition of the Orthodox Faith* 85. My translation. Cf. *Die Schriften des Johannes von Damaskos* (ed. B. Kotter, OSB; Patristische Texte und Studien, 12; Berlin & New York: W. de Gruyter, 1973), 190–1.

the Risen Christ, and in that Risen Christ the boundaries between death and life have been broken down, as has the separation implicit in our experience of space and time. As Alexander Schmemann has put it:

> Christianity is not reconciliation with death. It is the revelation of death, and it reveals death because it is the revelation of Life. Christ is this Life. And only if Christ is Life is death what Christianity proclaims it to be, namely the enemy to be destroyed, and not a 'mystery' to be explained.[7]

This also means that the distinction within the Christian community between the living and the departed is nullified; the communion in the Risen Christ transcends the separation of the living and the departed wrought by death.

Universal eschatology

The Orthodox Church lives in the hope of the coming again of Christ in glory, as the creed affirms, and of all that is bound up with this second coming: the Final Judgement, the resurrection of the dead, the transfiguration of the cosmos. All this is determined by the life on the threshold of the kingdom, experienced in the eucharistic celebration. This eschatological expectation, as we have seen, has implications for the nature of the Christian Church, gathered together as the Church to celebrate the Eucharist as an anticipation of the banquet of the kingdom. First and foremost, this means that the life of each individual Christian finds expression and meaning in the communion of the Church, and that the communion of the Church nurtures and fosters the life of each individual Christian. As Khomiakov expressed it, in a passage already cited in Chapter 6 (though in a different translation):

> We know that when any one of us falls, he falls alone; but no one is saved alone. He who is saved is saved in the Church, as a member of her, and in unity with all her other members. If anyone believes, he is in the communion of faith; if anyone loves, he is in the communion of love; if anyone prays, he is in the communion of prayer.[8]

---

[7] Alexander Schmemann, *The World as Sacrament* (London: Holt, Rinehart & Winston, 1966), 124.

[8] A. S. Khomiakov, *The Church Is One* (rev. trans. William Palmer, with an introductory essay by N. Zernov; London: Fellowship of St Alban & St Sergius, 1968), 38.

This conviction has implications both for the Final Judgement itself, and for the life we live in expectation of the coming of the kingdom. To anticipate what will be said later about individual eschatology, it lies behind the distinction drawn between the particular judgement of the individual, at the moment of death, and the universal Final Judgement with the coming of Christ, the *parousia*, at the end of time. As Fr Dumitru Stăniloae put it: the Final Judgement is additional to the particular judgement,

> because the full blessedness or damnation of each individual is organically bound up with the end of the world and the activity of humans within the world; that means therefore, that blessedness or damnation is dependent on the result of this activity, and that these results, whether good in the kingdom of God or evil in hell, have eternal consequences.[9]

It is for this reason that, as the eucharistic anaphora affirms, the eucharistic sacrifice is offered, first of all, for the Mother of God and the saints, for their blessedness will not be complete until the consummation of all human life at the last judgement.

This human coinherence has implications for life in expectation of the second coming. For while the coming of the kingdom with Christ's *parousia* is beyond any human expectation or preparation, nevertheless there is, to quote Stăniloae again, 'a deep and mysterious solidarity of Christ with the whole course of human life on earth'.[10] There is a parallel to this in the Eucharist: the holy gifts are *gifts*, not something we can ever demand or deserve, and yet truly to receive them and live out their power in our lives demands of each Christian an ascetic commitment, a commitment to fighting against anything in our lives opposed to Christ and nurturing everything that promotes love. St John Chrysostom remarks, 'for grace, if it is grace, saves those who want it, not those who do not choose it and reject it and fight against it continually and are opposed to it'.[11]

Furthermore, beyond the moral and ascetical demands, our life in expectation of the coming of the kingdom has political implications: to promote the values of the kingdom in the societies in which we

---

[9] Dumitru Stăniloae, *Orthodoxe Dogmatik* III (German trans. Hermann Pitters; Ökumenische Theologie, 16; Solothurn and Düsseldorf: Benziger, 1995), 292.

[10] Stăniloae, *Orthodoxe Dogmatik* III, 296.

[11] John Chrysostom, *Homily on Romans* 19 (ed. F. Field; Oxford: J. H. Parker, 1849), 320.

live 'between the times', or at least to seek to create a society in which the values of the kingdom are comprehensible. This will mean, in particular, striving against a culture of death and disposable life, a culture that arbitrarily limits its understanding of 'human life' to an undemanding 'norm' by excluding the impaired and handicapped, the not-fully formed and those with failing powers. It will also mean challenging human forms of society that impair the principle of human coinherence by favouring one part of society against others, whether this privilege is based on wealth, birth, race or occupation. So Berdyaev affirms: 'The fundamental principle of ethics may be formulated as follows: act so as to conquer death and affirm everywhere, in everything and in relation to everything, eternal and immortal life'.[12]

A central term in the Christian conception of the coming kingdom is the notion of *glory*: Christ will come in glory, the bodies of the blessed will be glorified, indeed the whole cosmos will be transfigured in glory. Various interpretations of this can be found in Orthodox theologians. For Fr Sergii Bulgakov, the second coming stands in contrast to Christ's first coming, in which he emptied himself of the divine glory and took on the form of a slave (Phil. 2.7): it is a manifestation in glory, as opposed to his first coming in *kenosis*, self-emptying. He sees a parallel to this in the period between Pentecost and the second coming – the period 'between the times' – where we find a *kenosis* of the Holy Spirit, for the Spirit is at work in the Church and the world in a hidden way – a hiddenness that will be revealed at the second coming. It is not just in the Church and human society that the Spirit is hidden, but in the whole natural world:

> The kenosis of the Holy Spirit that has descended into the world consists in a limitation of its gifts . . . The natural world retains its unchangingness in creaturely being; it remains in its unrealized and unfinished state. The fulness of its realization, its transparence for the Spirit, its appearance in glory, or glorification, are yet to come. This glorification depends not on a new coming of the Spirit, since the Spirit is already in the world, but on the fulness of its action. This fulness is the transfiguration of the world in connexion with the parousia; it is the new heaven and new earth into which Christ comes.

---

[12] Nicolas Berdyaev, *The Destiny of Man* (trans. Natalie Duddington; London: Centenary Press, 1945; first published 1937), 253.

In Scripture, the parousia is accompanied by the fire of the world, the destruction of the world, followed by its transfiguration, but this does not signify a succession or coincidence in time of two parallel events. It is one and the same event: the coming of Christ in glory and the revelation of glory to the world correspond to the action of the Holy Spirit . . . Pentecost's fiery tongues become the flame of the world fire, not consuming but transmuting the world. This figure represents a hieroglyph of the cosmic Pentecost. If the parousia is the second coming of Christ in the world, this time in glory, it is also the new revelation of the Holy Spirit, of God's glory, upon Christ and in the world. It is not a new coming of the Holy Spirit, for having come at Pentecost, the Holy Spirit does not leave the world but is hidden in the world, as it were.[13]

The transfiguration of the world at the second coming fulfils the 'groaning and travailing' of creation at the present time (Rom. 8.22); transfigured by glory, the cosmos will be manifest in its *beauty*, a beauty embracing both persons and things. To quote again from Stăniloae:

The radiant countenance of Christ will enlighten everyone and everything. Things will no more appear to be separated from persons, but as a possession common to all, as a means through which the love of Christ, of the angels and of humans, will come to light in an all-embracing pan-personalism of perfect community.[14]

Daringly, Berdyaev makes his point thus:

Paradise lies beyond good and evil and therefore is not exclusively the kingdom of 'the good' in our sense of the term. We come nearer to it when we think of it as beauty. The transfiguration and regeneration of the world is beauty and not goodness. Paradise is theosis, deification of the creature . . .[15]

and: 'My salvation is not only bound up with that of other men but also of animals, plants, minerals, every blade of grass – all must be transfigured and brought into the kingdom of God'.[16]

In the Last Judgement and transfiguration of the world, the one 'in whom all creation rejoices', the Blessed Virgin, has a special

---

[13] Bulgakov, *Bride*, 400.
[14] Stăniloae, *Orthodoxe Dogmatik* III, 323.
[15] Berdyaev, *Destiny*, 287.
[16] Berdyaev, *Destiny*, 294.

role to play. Because of her dormition and assumption, the Mother of God has anticipated the resurrection of the dead, and yet, as the troparion for the Feast of her Dormition proclaims, 'in falling asleep you did not abandon the world; . . . You passed over to life, for you are the Mother of Life.'[17] So in the second coming and judgement, the Mother of God appears with her son (as icons of the Last Judgement show), not as one to be judged, but pleading for sinners. Indeed, Bulgakov speculates, she *anticipates* her son's second coming in her manifestations to the saints, manifestations that have often been explicitly eschatological in character (such manifestations have not been confined to the Orthodox world: witness Lourdes and Fatima).[18]

Individual eschatology

'Individual eschatology' is concerned with the fate of the individual after death, and in particular, between the death of the individual and the Last Judgement. The Orthodox conception of this is based on the liturgical rites that accompany and follow the death of a Christian, informed by a theological understanding of what is involved in judgement and a sense of the communion of the living and the departed in the risen Christ: all supplemented by popular traditions expressed especially in the lives and experiences of the saints.

The Orthodox have a service – in essence, an abridged form of the funeral service – called by the Greeks the 'trisagion for the departed' and by the Russians the 'panikhida', that is celebrated on the third, ninth and fortieth days after the death of the departed. This threefold *post mortem* commemoration has its roots in ancient commemoration of the departed with lamentation and a communal meal on the third, ninth and thirtieth days, characteristic of the Mediterranean world (in the pre-Vatican II Latin missal, requiem masses were prescribed for the third, seventh and thirtieth days).[19] This service is also celebrated annually on the anniversary of the death. It consists of

---

[17] *An Orthodox Prayer Book* (Eng. trans. Archimandrite Ephrem Lash; Milton under Wychwood: St Alban & St Sergius, 2009), 105.

[18] Bulgakov, *Bride*, 409–15.

[19] Margaret Alexiou, *The Ritual Lament in Greek Tradition* (Cambridge: Cambridge University Press, 1974), 31–5.

prayers for the departed, the blessing of *kollyva* (a kind of cake of boiled wheat) and a lament for the departed – in the light of the resurrection, however, 'making our funeral lament a song: Alleluia, alleluia, alleluia', as one of the verses (the *ikos*) puts it.[20] The prayers for the departed make repeated petition for the departed souls that 'the Lord our God may establish their souls where the righteous rest' and keep them 'for the life of blessedness with you, O lover of mankind'.[21] These services enable the bereaved to give expression to their love and concern for the departed, and commend them into the hands of God the Creator, confident in their faith in the resurrection of Christ.

The period of forty days after death, punctuated by the third and the ninth day, is understood as setting out – in narrative form, as it were – what is involved in death and the passage to a period of waiting for the Last Judgement. The first three days are those in which the soul becomes accustomed to its separation from the body, a separation more or less difficult depending on how attached the soul had become to the body and earthly concerns.

The next six days constitute the period in which the soul is judged with respect to the virtues and vices that it has acquired in its earthly life. This period is represented as the passage through the 'toll-houses' or *telonia*, staffed, as it were, by an angel and a demon who between them determine the soul's fate. In its most elaborate form – in Blessed Theodora's *Life* of her spiritual father, Basil the Younger (tenth century) – there are 20 such toll-houses, at which the soul is examined over vain words, lies, calumnies, greed, laziness, theft, avarice, usury, injustice, envy, pride, anger, rancour, murder, magic, sexual impurity, adultery, sodomy, heresy, lack of compassion and cruelty of heart.[22] During this passage, the soul is assisted against the demons' efforts not just by the angels of the toll-houses, but also by its guardian angel, by the prayers of the saints and of those living on earth. The passage of the toll-houses represents vividly what is required for someone to pass from the sin and temptations of this world to the holy presence of God.

---

[20] *Orthodox Prayer Book*, 84.
[21] *Liturgy of St John Chrysostom*, 89, 88.
[22] Cf. Jean-Claude Larchet, *La vie après la mort selon la tradition orthodoxe* (Paris: Cerf, 2001), 109–19.

From the ninth day to the fortieth day, the soul is introduced to the other world and visits both the heavenly dwelling places and the abysses of hell, but even popular beliefs are extremely reticent over what all this involves. On the fortieth day, the soul undergoes the particular judgement, and then is assigned to an intermediate state, a state of waiting in Paradise or Hades, provisional in comparison with heaven and hell, that await the decisions of the Last Judgement. As to the nature of this intermediate state, Orthodox theology and even popular belief are again quite reticent, though the idea that in this intermediate state the soul is in a state of unconscious sleep finds little support, and any idea that the soul will experience further incarnations in its passage towards the Final Judgement (the idea of reincarnation or, more properly, metempsychosis), popular as this idea was in the Greco-Roman culture that first received Christianity, is firmly excluded. The question of the particular judgement and its distinction from the Final Judgement is an issue on which the Fathers of the Church do not speak with a single voice, but the prevailing view maintains a distinction between them.[23]

While this comparatively detailed account of the fate of the soul after death is often taken fairly literally by Orthodox believers, and not only at a popular level,[24] it has never been formally defined, and rests for its authority less on the Fathers of the Church than on popular belief, supported by liturgical practice. The essence of what is entailed by the services for the departed can, however, make good claim to formal Orthodox belief: that the departed are supported by the prayers of Christians, that the communion of living and departed has not been severed by death, that there is hope of 'a place of light, a place of refreshment, a place of repose, whence pain, sorrow and sighing have fled away' for the departed. The narrative details of the passage of the soul, for instance the toll-houses, are not, however, mentioned in these services, though the idea that death involves judgement and the inescapable realization of what we have made of our lives is.

---

[23] Cf. Larchet, *La vie*, 146–8.

[24] Cf. Nikolaos P. Vassiliadis, *The Mystery of Death* (trans. Fr Peter A. Chamberas; Athens: The Orthodox Brotherhood of Theologians, 1993); Archimandrite Seraphim Rose, *The Soul after Death* (Platina: St Herman of Alaska Brotherhood, 1995; first published 1980); and with some equivocation, Larchet, *La vie*.

The sequence of services – from the services for the dying Christian, to the commemoration on the fortieth day, and indeed annually – also serves a pastoral purpose, in assisting the bereaved to cope with their sense of loss and their sense of helplessness. The temporal dimension of the services may have more to do with the temporal process of bereaving and remembrance than with tracking the departed soul's progress in a state after death about which little has been revealed to us save God's sure love and Christ's triumph over death in his resurrection. What is to be affirmed, however, is that the comfort provided by these services and prayer for the departed rests on these truths, and is no mere placebo.

Problems in eschatology

We have already encountered various problems, and it is time to deal with them more directly. Such problems have long exercised Christians, but whereas in the West eventually solutions were found and generally accepted, in the East the questions remained, and remain, open, or at least continue to be discussed. Much of this discussion is bound up with the legacy of the great third-century Alexandrian theologian, Origen, to whom errors concerning both the first things (creation and fall) and the last things were attributed; he was condemned for them. In this section we shall think about four issues: (1) the notion of eternal damnation and, bound up with that, the nature of judgement; (2) the question of purgatory; (3) the nature of the resurrection body; and finally, (4) the question of universal salvation, or the final restoration of all (*apokatastasis pantôn*).

The notion of eternal damnation and the nature of judgement

The problem of eternal damnation is essentially how to reconcile such a notion with belief in God who 'is love' (1 John 4.16): what sense does it make to say that God is love and yet has created beings that are to be condemned to eternal damnation? The notion seems clearly affirmed in the Scriptures, indeed in some of the Lord's sayings in the Gospels (e.g. Matt. 22.30, 41, 46). For the most part, there has been great reluctance in the East, as in the West, to blunt the force of the words attributed to Christ about eternal damnation. The problem rather has been, how to understand them?

One way of approaching this issue focuses on the nature of judgement, picking up the ambivalence of the fourth Gospel about the judgement of Christ, the Son of Man, of whom it is said both that he came into the world for judgement (John 9.39) and that he did not come into the world to judge the world (John 3.17), and in the same breath: 'I judge no one, and yet if I judge, my judgement is true' (John 8.15–16). 'True' judgement is presumably judgement that is not arbitrary, but a recognition of the reality of the case.

It is along these lines that an influential tradition in Eastern theology interpreted judgement. The ultimate state of human beings, after the Final Judgement, is to behold the glory of God's love. For those whose inmost desire is longing for God, this will be ultimate fulfilment, ultimate bliss, but for those whose inmost desire is opposition to God – those who cry out, with Milton's Satan, 'Evil, be thou my good' – their inmost longing will be eternally frustrated, and they will experience eternal torment. St John Damascene, following St Maximos the Confessor, interprets judgement in such a way:

> For what is punishment, save the privation of what one longs for? According, therefore, to the analogy of desire, those who long for God rejoice, and those who long for sin are punished. And those who obtain what they long for rejoice in accordance with the measure of their longing, and those who fail suffer in accordance with the measure of their longing.[25]

Furthermore, according to John Damascene – in this following a suggestion of the fourth-century bishop, Nemesius of Emesa[26] – after death, the soul is unchangeably set in accordance with the fundamental orientation of its longing (the scrutiny of the toll-houses may be seen as a colourful way of assessing this fundamental orientation): a longing that has been refined and tested through life in the world. At the Last Judgement, this now-fixed orientation is recognized, and that is what is meant by judgement. If this is accepted, then it would appear that eternal damnation is theoretically possible, and is a recognition of the ultimate freedom of human beings, created in the image of God; such eternal damnation is experienced as ultimate

---

[25] John Damascene, *Against the Manichees* 75; cf. Maximos, *Questions to Thalassios* 59.
[26] Nemesius of Emesa, *On the Nature of Man* 1. 9–10 (trans. with an introduction and notes by R. W. Sharples and P. J. van der Eijk; Translated Texts for Historians, 49; Liverpool: Liverpool University Press, 2008, 44–5).

regret, as realizing that one is eternally loved by God, and yet no longer able either to accept or to reciprocate it (whether this is anything more than a theoretical possibility is another matter).

Purgatory

The notion of purgatory, as a kind of third place in the afterlife, alongside heaven and hell, has never had any place in Orthodox theology. The very words used by Greek theologians to designate this essentially Latin concept – *perkatorion* or *pourgatorion*, simple transliterations of the Latin word, *purgatorium* – rather than a genuine translation such as *katharterion*, bear witness to how foreign the notion seems. This is scarcely surprising, for it is generally accepted nowadays that, whatever precedents there may be for some process or experience of purification of the soul after death, the settled notion of a place, in some way equivalent to heaven or hell in the afterlife, only emerges in Latin theology as part of the theological revolution of the twelfth century.[27] The Orthodox East, therefore, encountered it as a strange innovation of Latin theology, to be imposed on them along with acceptance of the *Filioque* and papal supremacy as part of the cost of reunion in return for Western military support against the Turks. Not surprisingly, in such a context it was rejected.

Apart from the absence of such a notion in any accepted Fathers (Book 4 of St Gregory the Great's *Dialogues*, well known among Orthodox since the eighth century in Pope Zacharias' Greek translation, probably adumbrates the notion most clearly), the apparent suggestion that there was a third choice in the afterlife – other than heaven or hell – seemed to blunt the stark choice offered in the Gospels. If, however, the question about purgatory is broken down into its constituent parts, then the position becomes less clear. These constituent parts are: first, the question of a particular judgement; second, the question of the existence of a place, intermediate between heaven and hell, in the afterlife between death and the Last Judgement; and third, whether in this intermediate state souls undergo expiatory suffering, and in particular, whether this suffering takes place through the agency of fire.

---

[27] Jacques Le Goff, *The Birth of Purgatory* (trans. Arthur Goldhammer; London: Scolar Press, 1984).

First, as we have seen, the notion of a particular judgement after death is far from unacceptable in Orthodox theology. Second, the idea of an intermediate *state*, neither heaven nor hell, seems generally to be assumed in Orthodox belief about the afterlife, though to think of this state as a *place*, comparable with heaven and hell, is unusual. On the third question, the Orthodox position, though ambivalent, is more clearly negative. Does the scrutiny of the toll-houses imply that the soul undergoes purification before the Last Judgement? Perhaps, but as it stands it seems simply concerned with assessing the state of the departed soul. Orthodox set value on prayers for the departed souls, from which they must in some way benefit – by being purified? That any such purification involves suffering is again readily accepted, especially in view of the general belief that the soul, as it awaits the second coming, is not in a state of unconscious sleep.

That this suffering is expiatory is less clearly acceptable. What the Latins meant by expiatory suffering in purgatory is that by such suffering the soul renders satisfaction for sins forgiven: satisfaction meaning reparation for the effects of sins committed (mainly, per- haps, the effects on the soul of the sinner himself). Certainly in the past, some Orthodox theologians thought in terms of satisfaction (though historically the notion is much more characteristic of Western theology), and agreed that the suffering of the departed soul could render such satisfaction; others disagreed, and did not see 'fruits of repentance' as satisfaction, which might need to be made up after death. Again, historically, most Orthodox objections to purgatory were to the notion of purgatorial fire, often understood literally (as was the case with the Latins, too). In general, one could say that such 'scholastic' thinking, though common in seventeenth- and eighteenth-century Orthodox theologians, is uncommon nowadays.[28] The reti- cence that we found about how literally any detailed narrative of the fate of the soul after death is to be taken also covers the case of purgatory; the way in which a doctrine of purgatory is in danger of reifying a mysterious process in which souls of the departed, resting in the hands of God and supported by the prayers of the Church, are prepared for eternal bliss is to be avoided.

---

[28] On the debate in the seventeenth and eighteenth centuries, see Timothy Ware, *Eustratios Argenti: A Study of the Greek Church under Turkish Rule* (Oxford: Clarendon Press, 1964), 139–60.

The nature of the resurrection body

This – together with the question of the final restoration of all – was one of the issues for which Origen was historically condemned. In the fifth century there was attributed to him the teaching that the bodies of those raised at the resurrection of the dead would be spiritual – a doctrine he almost certainly did not hold. The central truth affirmed by the doctrine of the resurrection of the body is that human beings are not simply spiritual, but are constituted by both soul and body: a body on its own is a corpse, a soul on its own is one of the departed, human beings only exist as soul-and-body. The inclination, in the late classical culture in which Christianity first developed, to think of human life in essentially spiritual terms is to be resisted. At death, the body becomes a corpse; the gift of life in the kingdom of heaven means, in some sense, the restoration of the body.

In what sense? There is no doubt that the risen body will be different from human bodies as we know them. St Paul contrasts 'our humble body' with the 'body of [Christ's] glory' to which our body is to be conformed (Phil. 3.21); he also contrasts the body 'sown in corruption, . . . dishonour, . . . weakness', with the resurrection body, 'raised in incorruption, . . . glory, . . . power, . . . spiritual' (1 Cor. 15.42–44). The body of the risen Christ was both recognizable and unrecognized, occupying space, yet passing through locked doors. Origen insisted, rightly, that the risen body would be different from bodies as we know them and, following the apostle Paul, called them 'spiritual'. He was condemned because it was thought that such a 'spiritual body' would not be material, which was probably not what Origen meant.

In reaction against Origenism (and the spiritualism of a bastard Platonism), the Fathers insisted that the resurrection body would be, in important respects, continuous with this body; it would be the same body, raised up, not something quite different. The Fathers were well aware that the body is not an unchangeable entity – ingestion of food and excretion make this plain – but they were certainly not aware, as modern medical science reveals, of the extent to which the body changes its constituents over time. The question of the identity between the earthly and the risen body is clearly mysterious. All one can probably do is underline the extent to which the bodily cannot be elided from human identity. It is not just that we have souls *and* bodies, but rather that what we are, even our 'spiritual' capacities, is bound up with our bodies. We have already quoted Berdyaev's remark, 'The vision of another person's countenance, the expression of his eyes, can often be a spiritual revelation. The eyes, the gestures, the words – all these are infinitely more eloquent of a man's soul than of his body'.[29] It is because our sense of human identity involves both body and soul that some sort of continuity must exist between the earthly body and the risen body, if we are to say that, at the day of resurrection, we have been raised with Christ.

Universal salvation

Origen hoped for the 'restoration of all', *apokatastasis pantôn*, and this was certainly one of the reasons for his condemnation(s). His conviction did not simply rest on a philosophical belief that 'the end is like the beginning', a principle he affirmed several times in *On First Principles*. In one of his homilies on Leviticus, he asserted:

> We shall now see, how it is to be understood that our Saviour will drink wine no more until he drinks it anew with the saints in the kingdom of God. My Saviour even now weeps over my sins. My Saviour cannot rejoice, so long as I continue in iniquity. Why can he not? Because he himself is the advocate for my sins with the Father, as John his disciple says, 'for if anyone sins, we have an advocate with the Father, Jesus Christ, and he is the propitiation for our sins'. How, therefore, can he, who is the advocate for my sins, drink the wine of gladness, while I sadden him through my sinning? How could he be in gladness – he who draws near to the altar to offer sacrifice for me, a sinner; he, to whom sorrow returns without ceasing on account of my sins? I shall drink it with you, he says, in the kingdom of my Father. So long as we do not act so as to ascend to the kingdom, he cannot drink the wine alone, which he has promised to drink with us. He is there in sorrow, so long as I persist in error.[30]

Here we find a deeper reason for Origen's conviction of final restoration for all: for him it is inconceivable that Christ is to remain in

---

[29] Nicolas Berdyaev, *Solitude and Society* (trans. George Reavey; London: Centenary Press, 1938), 109.
[30] *Hom. in Levit.* 7. 2. Quoted in Stăniloae, *Orthodoxe Dogmatik* III, 296.

sorrow for all eternity, on account of the failure of any rational creature to respond to his love and benefit from his sacrifice.

Whereas in Western theology, such a conviction rapidly dies out (save for some women saints – 'tout un cortège des saintes femmes', as Hans Urs von Balthasar put it[31] – convinced that God's love could know no limit), in Orthodox theology hope in universal salvation, based on a conviction of the boundlessness of God's love, has never gone away. St Gregory of Nyssa interprets the apostle Paul's teaching that God will be 'all in all' (1 Cor. 15.28) to mean the 'complete annihilation of evil'.[32] St Maximos the Confessor likewise holds out the hope of the salvation of all. The grounds for this are principally the long-suffering love of God for all creation, and also the conviction that evil is without substance, but is rather a corruption or distortion of what is good. These two motives find striking expression in St Maximos' contemporary, St Isaac the Syrian, who asserts that

> there exists with [the Creator] a single love and compassion which is spread out over all creation, (a love) which is without alteration, timeless and everlasting . . . No part belonging to any single one of (all) rational beings will be lost, as far as God is concerned, in the preparation of that supernal kingdom[33]

and adds, quoting Diodore of Tarsus, 'not even the immense wickedness [of the demons] can overcome the measure of God's goodness'.[34] The pain of hell is the result of love: 'those who are punished in Gehenna are scourged by the scourge of love . . . For the sorrow caused in the heart by sin against love is more poignant than any torment'.[35] Evil and hell cannot be eternal: 'Sin, Gehenna and death do not exist at all with God, for they are effects, not substances. Sin is the fruit of free will. There was a time when sin did not exist, and there will be a time when it will not exist'.[36]

---

[31] Hans Urs von Balthasar, 'Actualité de Lisieux', *Thérèse de Lisieux: Conférences du Centenaire 1873–1973, Nouvelles* (1973, no. 2), 107–23, here 120–1.

[32] Gregory of Nyssa, *On the Soul and the Resurrection* 7.

[33] Isaac the Syrian, 'Part II', 40. 1, 7 (trans. Sebastian Brock, CSCO 555; Louvain: Peeters, 1995), 174, 176.

[34] Isaac, 'Part II', 39. 13 (trans. Brock), 169.

[35] Isaac, *Homily* 28, in *Ascetical Homilies of St Isaac the Syrian* (Boston, MA: Holy Transfiguration Monastery, 1984), 141.

[36] Isaac, *Homily* 27, 133.

This conviction that there is nothing outside God's loving care finds expression in the prayers of the Orthodox Church. In the service of kneeling at Vespers on the evening of Pentecost, we pray 'for those who are held fast in hell, granting us great hopes that there will be sent down from you to the departed repose and comfort from the pains which hold them'. This hope, amounting to a conviction, that there is nothing beyond the infinite love of God, that there is no limit to our hope in the power of his love, at least regards as a legitimate hope the universal salvation of all rational creatures, maybe even of the devil himself and his demons. Such a belief has found its defenders among modern Orthodox theologians, such as Olivier Clément,[37] Metropolitan Kallistos Ware[38] and Metropolitan Hilarion Alfeyev.[39] It was also the conviction of one of the greatest Orthodox saints of recent times, St Silouan of Athos, manifest in a conversation with another Athonite hermit, who declared 'with evident satisfaction',

'God will punish all atheists. They will burn in everlasting fire'.
Obviously upset, the Staretz said,
'Tell me, supposing you went to paradise, and there looked down and saw somebody burning in hell-fire – would you feel happy?'
'It can't be helped. It would be their own fault', said the hermit.
The Staretz answered with a sorrowful countenance:
'Love could not bear that', he said. 'We must pray for all'.[40]

---

[37] Olivier Clément, *The Roots of Christian Mysticism* (trans. Theodore Berkeley; London: New City Press, 1993), 296–307.

[38] Metropolitan Kallistos Ware, 'Dare We Hope for the Salvation of All?', in *The Collected Works*. Vol. 1, *The Inner Kingdom* (Crestwood, NY: St Vladimir's Seminary Press, 2000), 193–215.

[39] Metropolitan Hilarion Alfeyev, *The Mystery of Faith: An Introduction to the Teaching and Spirituality of the Orthodox Church* (trans. Jessica Rose; London: Darton, Longman & Todd, 2002), 212–23.

[40] Archimandrite Sophrony (Sakharov), *Saint Silouan the Athonite* (trans. Rosemary Edmonds; Essex: Patriarchal and Stavropegic Monastery of St John the Baptist, 1991), 48.

A guide to further reading

I have appended to this guide all the works I have cited or referred to in writing this book. It is a somewhat idiosyncratic selection, but that, I think, is in the nature of the case. As I said at the beginning, this is very much my introduction to Orthodox theology; it has no formal authority, if it convinces, it will convince by arousing interest.

For those who want a more formal introduction to Eastern Orthodox theology, I would mention a few volumes. First, Timothy (now Metropolitan Kallistos) Ware's book, *The Orthodox Church* (latest edn, London: Harmondsworth, 1993), is still the first place to go for an authoritative and concise account of the Orthodox Church and its beliefs. A more recent book, which I would warmly endorse, is John Anthony McGuckin, *The Orthodox Church: An Introduction to its History, Doctrine, and Spiritual Culture* (Oxford: Blackwell, 2008). There have recently been several encyclopedias and companions, such as *The Cambridge Companion to Orthodox Christian Theology* (ed. Mary B. Cunningham and Elizabeth Theokritoff; Cambridge: Cambridge University Press, 2008), *The Encyclopedia of Eastern Orthodox Christianity* (ed. John Anthony McGuckin; 2 vols; Oxford: Wiley-Blackwell, 2011) and *The Orthodox Christian World* (ed. Augustine Casiday; London & New York: Routledge, 2012). For an unparalleled brief introduction to the Orthodox theological vision, see John Behr, *The Mystery of Christ: Life in Death* (Crestwood, NY: St Vladimir's Seminary Press, 2006).

But beyond such basically introductory works, I would encourage the reading of the Fathers. There are two good series of translations of works of the Fathers: the *Popular Patristic Series* (Crestwood, NY: St Vladimir's Seminary Press), edited by Fr John Behr, and *Early Church Fathers* (now defunct, but still in print; London: Routledge), edited by Carol Harrison. And then the reading of Orthodox theologians of all ages, many of whom I have referred to in the course of the book.

I have made the practice and experience of prayer, both personal and public, central to my understanding of Orthodox theology. Perhaps I should mention some introductions to prayer from an Orthodox perspective, though one must quickly leave books behind one: Orthodox prayer is really very simple (though not necessarily easy) – standing before the icons, opening one's heart to God, and staying there. St Theophan the Recluse spoke of 'putting the mind in the heart, and standing before God'. A book on prayer based on his letters (for the most part) is *The Art of Prayer: An Orthodox Anthology* (compiled by Igumen Chariton of Valamo; trans. E. Kadloubovsky

160

and E. M. Palmer, with a valuable introduction by Timothy Ware; London & Boston: Faber, 1966). Other books I would recommend include: (now Archimandrite) Gabriel Bunge, *Earthen Vessels: The Practice of Personal Prayer according to the Patristic Tradition* (San Francisco: Ignatius Press, 2002); Metropolitan Kallistos Ware, *The Orthodox Way* (rev. edn; Crestwood, NY: St Vladimir's Seminary Press, 1999); two books by Metropolitan Anthony Bloom – *Living Prayer* and *School for Prayer* (London: Darton, Longmen & Todd, 1967, 1970) and Archimandrite Sophrony, *On Prayer* (Crestwood, NY: St Vladimir's Seminary Press, 1998).

List of books referred to

Scriptural and liturgical texts

I Agia Graphi (15th edn; Athens: Ekdosis Adelfotitos Theologon I «Zoi», 1999).

The Apocryphal Gospels (texts and trans. Bart D. Ehrman and Zlatko Plešu; Oxford: Oxford University Press, 2011).

Decrees of the Ecumenical Councils (ed. Norman P. Tanner SJ; 2 vols; London: Sheed & Ward, 1990).

The Divine Liturgy of our Father among the Saints Basil the Great (trans. Archimandrite Ephrem; privately published; Manchester: St Andrew's Press, 2001).

The Divine Liturgy of our Father among the Saints John Chrysostom (Oxford: Oxford University Press, 1995).

An Orthodox Prayer Book (Eng. trans. Archimandrite Ephrem Lash; Milton under Wychwood: Fellowship of St Alban & St Sergius, 2009).

Further translation of liturgical texts can be found on Archimandrite Ephrem's website: <www.anastasis.org.uk>.

There are translations of liturgical texts by Mother Maria and Metropolitan Kallistos Ware:

The Festal Menaion (London: Faber, 1969).

The Lenten Triodion (London: Faber, 1978).

The Lenten Triodion: Supplementary Texts (South Canaan: St Tikhon's Seminary Press, 2007).

Patristic texts

Clement of Alexandria (trans. G. W. Butterworth; Loeb Classical Library; London: Heinemann, 1919).

From Glory to Glory: Texts from Gregory of Nyssa (selected and introduced by Jean Daniélou; trans. and ed. Herbert Musurillo; London: John Murray, 1962).

Les Homélies catéchétiques de Théodore de Mopsueste (ed. Raymond Tonneau OP and Robert Devreesse; Studi e Testi, 145; Rome: Biblioteca Apostolica Vaticana, 1949).

Maximus Confessor, Selected Writings (trans. George C. Berthold; London: SPCK, 1985).

Nemesius of Emesa, *On the Nature of Man* (trans. with an introduction and notes by R. W. Sharples and P. J. van der Eijk; Translated Texts for Historians, 49; Liverpool: Liverpool University Press, 2008).

The Philokalia: The Complete Text (trans. G. E. H. Palmer, Philip Sherrard and Kallistos Ware; 4 vols out of 5; London & Boston: Faber & Faber, 1979–95).

Pseudo-Dionysius: The Complete Works (trans. Colm Luibheid; Mahwah, NJ: Paulist Press, 1987). A somewhat free translation. In many ways, John Parker's translation (*Dionysius the Areopagite* [London, 1897]), though quaint, is to be preferred.

St Athanasius, *On the Incarnation* (trans. with an introduction by John Behr, with an introduction by C. S. Lewis; Crestwood, NY: St Vladimir's Seminary Press, 2011). Available both with and without the Greek text.

St Basil the Great, *On the Holy Spirit* (trans. Stephen Hildebrand; Crestwood, NY: St Vladimir's Seminary Press, 2011).

St Basil the Great, *On the Human Condition* (trans. Nonna Verna Harrison; Crestwood, NY: St Vladimir's Seminary Press, 2005).

St Gregory Nazianzus, *Autobiographical Poems* (ed. and trans. Carolinne White; Cambridge Medieval Classics, 6; Cambridge: Cambridge University Press, 1996).

St Gregory Nazianzus, *On God and Christ, The Five Theological Orations and Two Letters to Cledonius* (trans. Frederick Williams and Lionel Wickham; Crestwood, NY: St Vladimir's Seminary Press, 2002).

St Gregory of Nyssa, *On the Soul and the Resurrection* (trans. Catharine P. Roth; Crestwood, NY: St Vladimir's Seminary Press, 1993).

St Gregory Palamas, *Défense des saints hésychastes* (introduction, critical text, translation and notes by Jean Meyendorff; 2 vols; 2nd edn; Louvain: Spicilegium Sacrum Lovaniense, 1973). Contains Greek text and French translation of the *Triads.*

St Gregory Palamas, *The One Hundred and Fifty Chapters* (ed. and trans. Robert E. Sinkewicz; Toronto: Pontifical Institute of Mediaeval Studies, 1988).

St Irenaeus of Lyons, *On the Apostolic Preaching* (trans. and ed. John Behr; Crestwood, NY: St Vladimir's Seminary Press, 1997).

St Isaac the Syrian, *Ascetical Homilies of St Isaac the Syrian* (Boston, MA: Holy Transfiguration Monastery, 1984).

St Isaac the Syrian, 'Part II' (trans. Sebastian Brock; CSCO, 555; Louvain: Peeters, 1995).

St John Chrysostom, *In Divi Pauli Epistolam ad Romanos Homiliae* XXXIII (ed. F. Field; Oxford: J. H. Parker, 1849).

St John of Damascus, *Against the Manichees, On the Two Wills of Christ* (ed. B. Kotter, OSB; *Die Schriften des Johannes von Damaskos*, IV. *Liber de haeresibus, Opera polemica* [Berlin & New York: W. de Gruyter, 1981]).

St John of Damascus, *Exposition of the Orthodox Faith* (ed. B. Kotter, OSB; *Die Schriften des Johannes von Damaskos*, Patristische Texte und Studien, 12; Berlin: W. de Gruyter, 1973).

St John of Damascus, *Three Treatises on the Divine Images* (trans. with an introduction by Andrew Louth; Crestwood, NY: St Vladimir's Seminary Press, 2003).

St John of Damascus, *Writings* (trans. Frederic H. Chase Jr; Fathers of the Church, 37; New York: Fathers of the Church, 1958).

St Maximos the Confessor, *Mystagogia* (ed. Christian Boudignon; CCSG, 69; Turnhout: Brepols, 2011).

St Maximos the Confessor, *On the Cosmic Mystery of Jesus Christ* (trans. Paul Blowers and Robert Louis Wilson; Crestwood, NY: St Vladimir's Seminary Press, 2003).

St Maximos the Confessor, *Opuscula exegetica duo* (ed. P. Van Deun; CCSG, 23; Turnhout: Brepols, 1991).

St Maximos the Confessor, *Quaestiones ad Thalassium* (ed. Carl Laga and Carlos Steel; CCSG, 7, 22; Turnhout: Brepols, 1980–90).

Theophilus of Antioch, *Ad Autolycum* (ed. and trans. Robert M. Grant; Oxford: Oxford University Press, 1970).

La Vie d'Étienne le Jeune par Étienne le Diacre (ed. Marie-France Auzépy; Aldershot: Valorium, 1996).

Other literature

Afanasiev, N., 'The Church's Canons: Changeable or Unchangeable?', in *Tradition Alive* (ed. Michael Plekon; Lanham, MD: University Press of America, 2003), 31–45.

Alexiou, Margaret, *The Ritual Lament in Greek Tradition* (Cambridge: Cambridge University Press, 1974).

Alfeyev, Metropolitan Hilarion, *The Mystery of Faith: An Introduction to the Teaching and Spirituality of the Orthodox Church* (trans. and ed. Jessica Rose; London: Darton, Longman & Todd, 2002).

Andreopoulos, Andreas, *The Sign of the Cross: The Gesture, the Mystery, the History* (Brewster, MA: Paraclete Press, 2006).

Balthasar, Hans Urs von, 'Actualité de Lisieux', in *Thérèse de Lisieux: Conférences du Centenaire 1873–1973, Nouvelles* (1973, no. 2), 107–23.

Balthasar, Hans Urs von, *Cosmic Liturgy: The Universe according to Maximus the Confessor* (San Francisco: Ignatius Press, 2003; German original 1941;

much expanded and re-written second edn 1961; Eng. trans. Brian E. Daley SJ from the 3rd German edn 1988).

Bartholomew, Ecumenical Patriarch, *On Earth as in Heaven: Ecological Vision and Initiatives of Ecumenical Patriarch Bartholomew* (ed. John Chryssavgis; New York: Fordham University Press, 2012).

Behr, John, *The Nicene Faith*, parts 1 & 2 (Crestwood, NY: St Vladimir's Seminary Press, 2004).

Behr, John, *The Way to Nicaea* (Crestwood, NY: St Vladimir's Seminary Press, 2001).

Berdyaev, Nicolas, *The Destiny of Man* (trans. Natalie Duddington; London: Centenary Press, 1937).

Berdyaev, Nicolas, *Solitude and Society* (trans. George Reavey; London: Greenwood Press, 1938).

Bulgakov, Sergius, *The Bride of the Lamb* (trans. Boris Jakim; Grand Rapids, MI: Eerdmans, 2002).

Bulgakov, Sergius, *A Bulgakov Anthology: Sergius Bulgakov 1871–1944* (ed. James Pain and Nicolas Zernov; London: SPCK, 1976).

Bulgakov, Sergius, *The Orthodox Church* (London: Centenary Press, 1935).

Bulgakov, Sergius, *Relics and Miracles: Two Theological Essays* (trans. Boris Jakim; Grand Rapids, MI: Eerdmans, 2011).

Bunge, Gabriel, *The Rublev Trinity* (Crestwood, NY: St Vladimir's Seminary Press, 2007).

Camelot, Th. OP, 'La théologie de l'image de Dieu', *Revue des Sciences philosophiques et théologiques* XL (1956), 443–71.

Clampitt, A., *The Collected Poems of Amy Clampitt* (New York: Knopf, 1997).

Clément, Olivier, *The Roots of Christian Mysticism* (trans. Theodore Berkeley; London: New City Press, 1993).

Crow, Gillian, *'This Holy Man': Impressions of Metropolitan Anthony* (London: Darton, Longman & Todd, 2005).

de la Taille, SJ, Maurice, *The Mystery of Faith and Human Opinion Contrasted and Defined* (London: Sheed & Ward, 1934).

du Boulay, Juliet, *Cosmos, Life, and Liturgy in a Greek Orthodox Village* (Limni, Greece: D. Harvey, 2009).

Eliot, T. S., *Four Quartets* (London: Faber & Faber, 1944).

Eliot, T. S., *Selected Essays* (London: Faber & Faber, 1963).

Florensky, Pavel, *The Pillar and Ground of the Truth: An Essay in Orthodox Theodicy in Twelve Letters* (trans. Boris Jakim; Princeton, NJ: Princeton University Press, 1997).

Gallaher, Brandon, 'Graced Creatureliness: Ontological Tension in the Uncreated/ Created Distinction in the Sophiologies of Solov'ev, Bulgakov and Milbank', *Logos: A Journal of Eastern Christian Studies* 47 (2006), 163–90.

Hayward, C. T. R., *Jerome's Hebrew Questions on Genesis* (Oxford: Clarendon Press, 1995).

Hengel, Martin, *The Septuagint as Christian Scripture* (Edinburgh: T. & T. Clark, 2002).

Jakim, Boris, and Robert Bird (trans. and ed.), *On Spiritual Unity: A Slavophile Reader* (Hudson, NY: Lindisfarne Books, 1998).

Jones, David, *The Anathemata* (2nd edn; London: Faber & Faber, 1955).

Jones, David, *Epoch and Artist* (London: Faber & Faber, 1959).

Kamesar, Adam, *Jerome, Greek Scholarship and the Hebrew Bible* (Oxford: Clarendon Press, 1993).

Khomiakov, A. S., *The Church Is One* (rev. trans. William Palmer, with an introductory essay by N. Zernov; London: Fellowship of St Alban & St Sergius, 1968).

Larchet, Jean-Claude, *La vie après la mort selon la tradition orthodoxe* (Paris: Cerf, 2001).

Le Goff, Jacques, *The Birth of Purgatory* (trans. Arthur Goldhammer; London: Scolar Press, 1984).

Lewis, C. S., *Mere Christianity* (London: Fontana Books, 1959).

Lossky, Vladimir, *The Mystical Theology of the Eastern Church* (London: James Clarke & Co., 1957).

Louth, Andrew, 'Eastern Orthodox Eschatology', in *The Oxford Handbook of Eschatology* (ed. Jerry L. Walls; Oxford and New York: Oxford University Press, 2008), 233–47.

Louth, Andrew, 'The Fathers on Genesis', in *The Book of Genesis, Composition, Reception, and Interpretation* (ed. Craig A. Evans, Joel N. Lohr and David L. Petersen; Leiden: Brill, 2012), 561–78.

Louth, Andrew, *Greek East and Latin West: The Church AD 681–1071* (Crestwood, NY: St Vladimir's Seminary Press, 2007).

Louth, Andrew, 'Inspiration of the Scriptures', *Sobornost* 31.1 (2009), 29–44.

Louth, Andrew, 'Pagans and Christians on Providence', in *Texts and Culture in Late Antiquity: Inheritance, Authority and Change* (ed. J. H. D. Scourfield; Swansea: Classical Press of Wales, 2007), 279–97.

Louth, Andrew, *St John Damascene: Tradition and Originality in Byzantine Theology* (Oxford: Oxford University Press, 2002).

Louth, Andrew, 'Wisdom and the Russians: The Sophiology of Fr Sergei Bulgakov', in *Where Shall Wisdom Be Found?* (ed. Stephen C. Barton; Edinburgh: T. & T. Clark, 1999), 169–81.

Müller, Mogens, *The First Bible of the Church: A Plea for the Septuagint* (Journal for the Study of the Old Testament: Supplement Series, 206; Sheffield: Sheffield Academic Press, 1996).

Newman, J. H., *An Essay on the Development of Christian Doctrine* (The Edition of 1845; ed. J. M. Cameron; Harmondsworth: Penguin, 1974).

Obolensky, Dimitri, *The Byzantine Commonwealth: Eastern Europe 500–1453* (London: Weidenfeld & Nicolson, 1971).

Metropolitan Philaret of Moscow, *Catechism of the Orthodox Church* (repr., Willits, CA, n.d.).

Philaret (Drozdov) of Moscow, *Izbrannye Trudy Pisma Vospominaniya* (Moscow: St Tikhon's Orthodox Theological Institute, 2003).

Plato's Phaedo (trans. R. Hackforth; Cambridge: Cambridge University Press, 1972).

Pleşu, Andrei, *Actualité des anges* (Paris: Buchet Chastel, 2003).

Rilke, Rainer Maria, *Das Buch der Bilder* (Leipzig: Insel-Verlag, 1931).

Rose, Archimandrite Seraphim, *The Soul after Death* (Platina: St Herman of Alaska Brotherhood, 1995; first published 1980).

Schmemann, Alexander, *The Historical Road of Eastern Orthodoxy* (London: Holt, Rinehart & Winston, 1963).

Schmemann, Alexander, *The World as Sacrament* (London: Darton, Longman & Todd, 1966; originally called, and now universally available as, *For the Life of the World*).

Sherrard, Philip, *Christianity: Lineaments of a Sacred Tradition* (Brookline, MA: Holy Cross Orthodox Press, 1997).

Shoemaker, Stephen J., *Ancient Traditions of the Virgin Mary's Dormition and Assumption* (Oxford: Oxford University Press, 2002).

Archimandrite Sophrony (Sakharov), *Saint Silouan the Athonite* (trans. Rosemary Edmonds; Essex: Patriarchal and Stavropegic Monastery of St John the Baptist, 1991).

Stăniloae, Dumitru, *Orthodoxe Dogmatik* (German trans. Hermann Pitters; 3 vols; Solothurn and Düsseldorf: Benziger, 1984–95). This is coming out rather slowly in an English translation as *The Experience of God* (3 vols so far; Brookline, MA: Holy Cross Orthodox Press, 1994–).

Thekla, Mother, *The Monastery of the Assumption: A History* (Library of Orthodox Thinking, pamphlet no. 8; Whitby: Greek Orthodox Monastery of the Assumption, 1984).

Vassiliadis, Nikolaos P., *The Mystery of Death* (trans. Fr Peter A. Chamberas; Athens: The Orthodox Brotherhood of Theologians, 1993).

Ware, Metropolitan Kallistos, *The Collected Works.* Vol. 1, *The Inner Kingdom* (Crestwood, NY: St Vladimir's Seminary Press, 2000).

Ware, Timothy, *Eustratios Argenti: A Study of the Greek Church under Turkish Rule* (Oxford: Clarendon Press, 1964).

Yannaras, Christos, *Elements of Faith: An Introduction to Orthodox Theology* (Edinburgh: T. & T. Clark, 1991).

Yannaras, Christos, *The Freedom of Morality* (Crestwood, NY: St Vladimir's Seminary Press, 1984).

Zizioulas, John D., *Communion and Otherness* (London: T. & T. Clark, 2006).

Zizioulas, Metropolitan John of Pergamon, 'The Eucharist and the Kingdom of God', *Sourozh* 58 (November 1994), 1–12; 59 (February 1995), 22–38; 60 (May 1995), 32–46.

Index

167

Index